Collins

Easy Learning

KS3 Maths Revision

Levels 3-6

Keith Gordon

About this book

This book has been written to help you prepare for your Key Stage 3 Maths Test at the end of Year 9. It contains all the content you need to do well in the two written papers and the mental test.

The book is divided into four sections which correspond to the four areas of assessment (Attainment Targets) in the National Curriculum.

Each topic is contained within a double page. The left-hand page has all the information and the right-hand page has worked examples of Test questions (including mental test questions) to show how the information can be applied in the Test.

The information boxes have been given approximate National Curriculum levels to show you what level the topic is. You still need to know all of the lower level information, even if you are working at a higher level.

Special features

- **Spot Check questions** on every double page are a quick way to check that you've taken in the key points. You can find the answers to these on the inside back cover.

- **Top Tips** give extra advice and pick out key facts to help with your revision.

- **Did You Know?** items are there just for fun and a bit of light relief.

Revision and practice

Use this book alongside Collins *Easy Learning KS3 Maths Workbook Levels 3–6*. The workbook contains Test-style questions and practice papers so you can check that you have learnt and understood everything from this revision book.

Jenny Turner
8 Wharfedale Crescent
Garforth
LS25 1LD
Tel: 07787 575570
Em: jennyturner@phonecoop.coop

510   £4.99

ISBN-13 978-0-00-723349-6
ISBN-10 0-00-723349-3

Keith Gordon asserts his moral right to be identified as the author of this work.

British Library Cataloguing in Publication Data
A Catalogue record for this publication is available from the British Library

Written by Keith Gordon
Design by Andy Summers, Planet Creative Ltd
Illustrations by Kathy Baxendale, Jerry Fowler, David Whittle
Index compiled by Jane Read
Printed and bound in Malaysia by Imago

Contents

Answers to Spot Check questions are on the inside back cover.

NUMBER Place value

Hundreds, tens and units

- **Place value** is the value of a digit in a number depending on its **position** in the number. The number 562 is 500 + 60 + 2, so in columns it is:

Hundreds	Tens	Units
5	6	2

Top Tip!
You can say 500 or 100 for the value of the 5. 500 is better.

Example: Write the number 2057 in words.
Two thousand and fifty-seven.

Example: Here are 4 number cards. 9 4 8 2

    a What is the smallest even number you can make with the cards?
    b What is the largest odd number you can make with the cards?
    c Use two of the cards to make numbers as close as possible to the numbers below. The first one has been done for you.

    i 4 9 → 5 0   **ii** 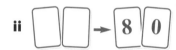 → 8 0   **iii** 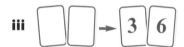 → 3 6

    a 2498   *b* 8429   *c ii* 82 *iii* 42

Top Tip!
The closest number could be bigger or smaller. Work out the difference between the numbers.

Decimals

- Numbers smaller than a unit are called **decimal fractions**. The **decimal point** separates the whole numbers from the decimal fractions.

The number 17.34 is 10 + 7 + 0.3 + 0.04, so in columns it is:

Tens	Units	.	Tenths	Hundredths
1	7	.	3	4

Top Tip!
If you are giving an amount of money in pounds and pence always write down 2 decimal places. £3.6 for £3.60 will be marked wrong.

The number of digits after the decimal point is the number of **decimal places** the number has.

Example: Here are some cards. 1 2 5 6 .

    a Use three of the cards to make a number between 2 and 3.

    b Use four of the cards to make a number between 1.5 and 1.6.

    a 2.1, 2.5 or 2.6   *b* 1.52 or 1.56

How many tenths are there in 1.3?

One tenth

Write the number 'two thousand and four' in figures.

2004

a Write a number that is bigger than one thousand but smaller than one thousand and fifty. Give your answer in figures.

b Write a one decimal place number that is bigger than zero but smaller than a half.

Answers
a *Any number from 1001 to 1049.*
b *0.1, 0.2, 0.3 or 0.4*

Did You Know?

The Dewey Decimal Classification system, devised by Melvil Dewey in the 1870s, is used to classify library books.

Spot Check

1 Write the numbers 1.3, 1.02, 1.2 and 1.324 in order with the smallest first.

2 3 6 4 5 ·

Use the cards to

a write the biggest odd number you can
b write a three-digit even number bigger than 600
c write a number between 5 and 5.5
d write a number that is 10 times bigger than 0.36

Addition and subtraction

- You can use a **blank number line** or **column methods** for addition and subtraction.

Example: Work out 1056 + 309

```
        +300          +9
```
1056   1356   1365

So 1056 + 309 = 1365

Example: Work out 6523 – 670

$$
\begin{array}{r}
{}^5\!\!\!\not6\;{}^{14}\!\!\!\not5\;{}^1\!2\;3 \\
-\quad\;6\;7\;0 \\
\hline
5\;8\;5\;3
\end{array}
$$

Top Tip!

If you use column methods make sure you line up the units column.
This type of question will be on Paper 1. Always show the carry and borrowing digits.

Multiplication and division

- You can do short multiplication and division in columns or break it down into bits.

Example: Work out **a** 453 x 6 **b** 372 x 4

a
$$
\begin{array}{r}
4\;5\;3 \\
\times\qquad 6 \\
\hline
2\,{}_3 7\,{}_1 8
\end{array}
$$

b
$$
\begin{array}{rr}
4 \times 300 = & 1\;2\;0\;0 \\
4 \times 70 = & 2\;8\;0 \\
4 \times 2 = & 8 \\
\hline
& 1\;4\;8\;8
\end{array}
$$

Example: Work out **a** 182 ÷ 7 **b** 655 ÷ 5

a
$$
\begin{array}{r}
2\;6 \\
7\overline{)1\;8\;{}^4 2}
\end{array}
$$

b
$$
\begin{array}{rr}
600 \div 5 = & 120 \\
50 \div 5 = & 10 \\
5 \div 5 = & 1 \\
\hline
& 131
\end{array}
$$

Top Tip!

The 1, 2, 5 and 10 times tables are fairly easy to remember. The 9 times table can be done using your fingers, e.g. 4 x 9. Hold your hands up and fold down the fourth finger.

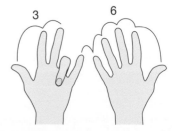

There are 3 fingers before the folded finger and 6 after it. 4 x 9 = 36

Spot Check

1 Work out
a 632 + 24   **b** 9970 – 880
c 7 x 82   **d** 8 x 67
e 312 ÷ 6   **f** 884 ÷ 5

What is the remainder when 37 is divided by 8?

4 x 8 = 32, so 37 = 4 x 8 + 5. The remainder is 5.

What is 6 x 35?

6 x 30 = 180, 6 x 5 = 30, 180 + 30 = 210

level
4

Sample National  Test question

Look at the sign for a car park.

Car Park
35p for 15 minutes

How much does it cost to park for an hour?

Answer
There are lots of ways to do these calculations but always show your method.
There are 4 lots of 15 minutes in one hour so the calculation is 4 x 35.

4 x 30 = 120
4 x   5 =   20
———————————————
4 x 35 = 140

So it costs 140p or £1.40 to park for one hour.

Ordering decimals

• When you put decimals in order, first compare the whole numbers, then the tenths, then the hundredths and then the thousandths.

Example: Which is bigger 1.24 or 1.6?

Compare 1.24 and 1.60.
1.60 is greater than 1.24.

> **Top Tip!**
> Give both numbers the same number of decimal places by adding zeros.

Example: Freddy, Mary and Alice are members of a family.
Freddy is 1.36 metres tall.
Mary is 1.5 metres tall.
Alice is 0.98 metres tall.

a Put the children in order of size with the smallest first.

a Write all the heights with the same number of decimal places.
Freddy 1.36, Mary 1.50, Alice 0.98
The order of size is: Alice, Freddy, Mary.

b Another child, Ben, is 0.5 metres shorter than Freddy.
How tall is Ben?

b 1.36 − 0.5 = 0.86 metres

Adding and subtracting decimals

• Adding and subtracting decimals is just like normal addition and subtraction. All you have to do is **line up the decimal point**.

Example: 1.23 + 3.4

```
  1 . 2 3
+ 3 . 4 0
---------
  4 . 6 3
```

Example: 3.4 − 1.68

```
  ²3̶ . ¹³4̶ ¹0
- 1 . 6 8
-----------
  1 . 7 2
```

> **Top Tip!**
> Add zeros here to fill the columns.

Spot Check

1 Put the following decimals in order from the smallest to the largest: 2.3, 1.89, 0.645

2 Add 0.5 to 1.8

3 Subtract 1.8 from 5.2

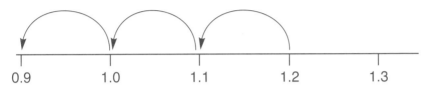
What is 1.2 − 0.3?

Think of a number line and count backwards.

0.9	1.0	1.1	1.2	1.3

1.2 − 0.3 = 0.9

levels
3-4

Sample National 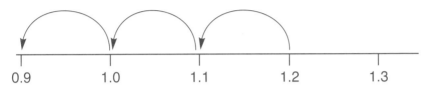 Test question

a   Rick buys a cassette, a CD and a DVD.
      How much does he pay altogether?

b   What is the difference between the cost of a CD and a DVD?

   £3.99      £9.49      £15.35

Answers
Write the numbers in a column with the decimal points lined up.

a
```
    3 . 9 9
    9 . 4 9
+  1 5 . 3 5
 ─────────────
  2 8 . 8 3
 1   1   2
```

He pays £28.83 altogether.

b
```
  ¹⁴  ¹²  ¹
  1 5 . 3 5
−   9 . 4 9
 ─────────────
    5 . 8 6
```

The difference is £5.86.

National Test questions usually put the question into a real-life situation.

This type of question will be on Paper 1.

Did You Know?
The first mathematician to use the idea of decimals was Aryabhata, who lived in India between 476 and AD 550.

NUMBER

Long multiplication and division

Long multiplication

• There are many ways of doing long multiplication. Two are shown here.

The **standard column** method.

Example: Work out 32 × 256

```
        2 5 6
  x       3 2
        5 1 2
  + 7 6 8 0
      8 1 9 2
```

The **box method**.

Example: Work out 43 × 264

X	200	60	4
40	8000	2400	160
3	600	180	12

Add up the numbers in the boxes.

```
      8 0 0 0
      2 4 0 0
        1 6 0
        6 0 0
        1 8 0
  +         1 2
      1 1 3 5 2
```

Top Tip!

Decide which method you prefer and stick with it.

Long division

• There are two ways of doing long division.

The **standard column** method.

Example: Work out 962 ÷ 37

```
          2 6
  3 7 | 9 6 2
    -   7 4
        2 2 2
    -   2 2 2
            0
```

The repeated subtraction or '**chunking**' method.

Example: Work out 896 ÷ 28

```
      8 9 6
  -   5 6 0      20 x 28
      3 3 6
  -   2 8 0      10 x 28
        5 6
  -       5 6      2 x 28
          0      32 x 28
```

Top Tip!

National Test questions usually ask part **a** as a long multiplication and part **b** as a long division and put the question into a real-life situation.

Top Tip!

Write out some of the easier times tables for the divisor:

1 x 28 =   28
2 x 28 =   56
4 x 28 = 112
10 x 28 = 280
20 x 28 = 560

Subtract the biggest multiple you can each time.

 **pot Check**

1 Work out 37 x 52

2 Work out 918 ÷ 17

Sample National Test question

a A garden centre has 576 winter pansies for sale.
Each plant costs 28p.
How much will all 576 cost?

b The pansies are packed in trays of 18.
How many trays does the garden centre have?

Answers

a *This is done by the box method.*
The total is £161.28.

X	500	70	6
20	10000	1400	120
8	4000	560	48

```
  1 0 0 0 0
    1 4 0 0
      1 2 0
    4 0 0 0
      5 6 0
+       4 8
 1 6 1 2 8
```

Top Tip!

Estimate the answer as a
check on your working:
28 x 576p
Round this to 30 x 600p
= 18 000p
= £180

b *This is done by the standard method.*
They have 32 trays.

```
       3 2
18 | 5 7 6
   - 5 4 0
     ─────
       3 6
   -   3 6
     ─────
         0
```

Top Tip!

Check an answer to a division by
multiplying by the original divisor:

18 x 32 =
10 x 30 = 300
10 x 2 = 20
 8 x 30 = 240
 8 x 2 = 16
        ─────
          576

Did You Know?

The oldest surviving calculating
aid is the Salamis tablet
which was used in 300 BC.
It is now in the National
Museum in Athens.

NUMBER

Rounding and approximation

levels 3-4

Rounding to nearest 10, 100 etc.

• Most numbers used in everyday life are rounded. For example, the size of football crowds, the values of companies etc.

Example: Round the following numbers to **i** the nearest 10 **ii** the nearest 100

  a 238   **b** 1945

  a i 238 is 240 to the nearest 10 **ii** 200 to the nearest 100

  b i 1945 is 1950 to the nearest 10 **ii** 1900 to the nearest 100

> **Top Tip!**
> If a number is halfway between two possible values, such as 45, then round upwards to 50.

levels 3-4

Rounding to decimal places

• The number of **decimal places** a number has is the **number of non-zero digits after the decimal point** (zeros directly after the point count).

  For example, 17.32 has 2 decimal places, 3.005 has 3 decimal places and 0.0802 has 4 decimal places.

Example: Round the following numbers to **i** 2 decimal places **ii** 1 decimal place

  a 3.672   **b** 0.239

  a i 3.672 is 3.67 to 2 decimal places **ii** 3.7 to 1 decimal place

  b i 0.239 is 0.24 to 2 decimal places **ii** 0.2 to 1 decimal place

> **Top Tip!**
> When you have a decimal answer you don't have to round it off unless the question asks you to.

levels 3-4

Rounding to 1 significant figure

• The number of **significant figures** a number has is the **number of non-zero digits** (zeros between digits count as significant figures).

  For example, 1700 has 2 significant figures, 3005 has 4 significant figures and 0.08 has 1 significant figure.

• You only need to be able to round numbers to 1 significant figure.

Example: Round the following numbers to 1 significant figure.

  a 2672   **b** 0.38   **c** 4.92   **d** 112

  a 2672 is 3000

  b 0.38 is 0.4

  c 4.92 is 5

  d 112 is 100

> **Top Tip!**
> The abbreviation for decimal places is d.p. and s.f. for significant figures.

 **Spot Check**   **1** Find approximate answers to **a** 178 x 32 **b** 306 ÷ 48

Approximations

- It is useful to be able to approximate the answer to calculations. This way you can check if your answers are correct.

Example: By rounding the numbers to 1 significant figure find an approximate answer to

$$\frac{312 \times 58.2}{19.3}$$

Rounding the numbers to 1 significant figure makes the calculation $\frac{300 \times 60}{20}$

20 goes into 60 three times so the calculation becomes $300 \times 3 = 900$

An approximate answer is 900.

Top Tip!

This type of question will be on Paper 1 but you can always use approximations to make sure answers are sensible on both papers.

Sample mental test question

The length of a piece of wood is given as 80 cm to the nearest 10 centimetres. What is the smallest possible length it could be?

To the nearest 10 the smallest length it could be is 75 cm.

Sample National Test question

The lengths of these rivers are shown in the following table.

River	Length (km)	To nearest 10 km	To nearest 100 km
Thames	346		
Shannon	323		
Severn	355		

a Complete each column.

b Another river is described as being 290 km to the nearest 10 km and 300 km to the nearest 100 km.

   i Could the river be 296 km in length?

   ii What is the shortest length it could be?

Answers

a

River	Length (km)	To nearest 10 km	To nearest 100 km
Thames	346	350	300
Shannon	323	320	300
Severn	355	360	400

b **i** *No 296 would be 300 to the nearest 10*

   ii *285 km*

Did You Know?

The longest river in the world is the Amazon, which is about 6500 km long.

NUMBER

Multiplying and dividing decimals

Multiplying by powers of 10

- When you **multiply** by **10** all the digits move **one** place to the **left**. When you **multiply** by **100** all the digits move **two** places to the **left**.

Example: Work out **a** 2.79 x 10 **b** 3.2 x 100

a

Tens	Units	.	Tenths	Hundredths
	2	.	7	9
x 10 2	7	.	9	

b

Hundreds	Tens	Units	.	Tenths	Hundredths
		3	.	2	
x 100 3	2	0	.		

- You will need to add a zero in part **b** and you do not have to put in the decimal point for a whole number.

Dividing by powers of 10

- When you **divide** by **10** all the digits move **one** place to the **right**. When you **divide** by **100** all the digits move **two** places to the **right**.

Example: Work out **a** 32.4 ÷ 10 **b** 2.7 ÷ 100

a

Tens	Units	.	Tenths	Hundredths
3	2	.	4	
÷ 10	3	.	2	4

b

Units	.	Tenths	Hundredths	Thousands
2	.	7		
÷ 100 0	.	0	2	7

- You will need to add a zero before and after the decimal point in part **b**.

> **Top Tip!**
> Remember it's the digits that move when multiplying, not the decimal point.

Multiplying and dividing decimals

- Multiplying and dividing decimals is just like normal multiplying and dividing. All you have to do is keep the decimal point lined up.
- The decimal point in the answer is always underneath the decimal point in the question.

Example: Work out 3.76 x 4

```
    3 . 7 6
  x       4
  1 5 . 0 4
      3 2
```

Example: Work out 8.04 ÷ 6

```
      1 . 3 4
  6 | 8 .²0 ²4
```

> **Top Tip!**
> Estimate the answer just to be sure.
> 3.76 x 4 is approximately 4 x 4 = 16
> 8.04 ÷ 6 is approximately 9 ÷ 6 = 1.5

Sample National 💡 Test questions

a A shop sells boxes of chocolates for £3.38.
How much do 10 boxes cost?

£3.38

b A box of 6 Easter eggs costs £16.20.
How much does each egg cost?

£16.20

Answers

a *Move the digits one place to the left 3.38 x 10 = 33.8*
10 boxes will cost £33.80.

b

```
      2 . 7 0
6 | 1 6 .⁴2 0
```
  Each egg costs £2.70.

Top Tip!

Don't forget to put a zero on the end as the answer is in pounds and pence.

Top Tip!

Don't forget to estimate:
16.20 ÷ 6 ≈ 18 ÷ 6 = 3
'Is approximately equal to' can be shown by this symbol: ≈

Did You Know?

The world's most expensive Easter egg is the $24 million Fabergé Coronation Egg.

🔍 **Spot Check**   **1** Work out   **a** 0.7 x 100   **b** 4.52 ÷ 10   **c** 3.12 x 6   **d** 7.35 ÷ 5

Adding and subtracting negative numbers

Example: Work out +5 – 7

- Use a number line. Starting at zero, first move 5 units to the right, and then move 7 units to the left.

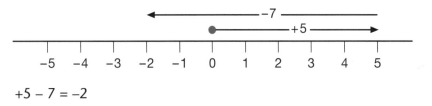

+5 – 7 = –2

> **Top Tip!**
> Always start at zero. Count to the **left** for **negative** numbers and to the **right** for **positive** numbers.

- Sometimes calculations have two plus or minus signs occurring together.

Example: Work out **a** –5 + –6 **b** –8 – –9

a

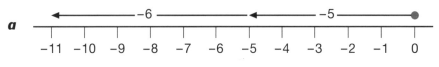

–5 + –6 = –11

b This is the same as –8 + 9.

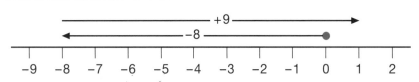

–8 – –9 = +1

> **Top Tip!**
> You must be very careful when two minus signs occur together.
> **Two minus** signs **together** act as a **plus**. So +8 – –5 is the same as +8 + 5 = 13.

Multiplying and dividing negative numbers

- Multiplying and dividing negative numbers is just like normal multiplying and dividing. All you have to do is combine the signs together correctly.

Example: Work out **a** –3 × +4 **b** –12 ÷ –2

- The rules for the signs are the same as above: + and – give a – answer; – and – give a + answer.
    a –3 × +4 is the same as – +3 × 4 = –12
    b –12 ÷ –2 is the same as – –12 ÷ 2 = +6

> **Top Tip!**
> When signs are **different** the answer will be **negative**. When signs are the **same** the answer will be **positive**.

Spot Check   **1** Work out **a** –7 + –2 **b** +3 – –6 **c** –3 × –4 **d** +15 ÷ –3

What number is 5 less than –3?

As this is a mental question you will have to picture a number line in your head to get an answer of –8.

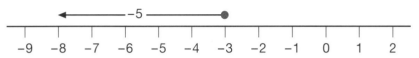

level
6

Sample National Test questions

1   The temperature at midnight in Edinburgh was –5 °C and at midday it was 7 °C.
By how many degrees did the temperature increase from midnight to midday?

2   You have these number cards.

a   Pick two cards to make the following calculations true.

i .... + ... = 5   **ii** .... – .... = –3   **iii** .... ÷ .... = –2

b   Pick two cards to make the answer to the following as large as possible.

☐ X ☐ = ...

Answers
1   *From –5 to +7 is a difference of 12 °C.*
2   *Try different combinations of the cards.*
   a i *6 + –1 = 5*   **ii** *–1 – 2 = –3*   **iii** *6 ÷ –3 = –2*
   b *–5 x –3 = +15*

Top Tip!

National Test questions test if you understand the idea of negative numbers. Remember the rules!

Did You Know?

The lowest temperature recorded was –89.4 °C in Vostok, Russia, in 1983 and the highest was 59.4 °C in Libya in 1922.

NUMBER

Adding and subtracting fractions

Cancelling fractions

- **Cancelling** fractions means looking for a **common factor** on the top and bottom of the fraction.
- Divide both the top number (**numerator**) and the bottom number (**denominator**) by the common factor.

  Once you've done this, the fraction is in its 'simplest form' or 'lowest terms'.

Example: Cancel the fraction $\frac{15}{20}$ to its simplest form.

15 and 20 have a highest common factor of 5.

$$\frac{15 \div 5}{20 \div 5} = \frac{3}{4}$$ We write this as: $\frac{\cancel{15}^3}{\cancel{20}_4}$

Top Tip!

Look for the largest number that divides into both the numerator and the denominator.

Adding fractions

- You can only add and subtract fractions if they have the same denominator.

Example: Add $\frac{2}{3} + \frac{3}{4}$

First, find the **lowest common multiple** of the two denominators, 3 and 4. The lowest common multiple is the smallest number in the 3 and 4 times table. This is 12.

Now make both fractions into twelfths.

$\frac{2}{3} = \frac{8}{12}$ (Multiply top and bottom by 4)

$\frac{3}{4} = \frac{9}{12}$ (Multiply top and bottom by 3)

Then just add the numerators and leave the denominator unchanged.

$$\frac{2}{3} + \frac{3}{4} = \frac{8}{12} + \frac{9}{12} = \frac{17}{12}$$

A fraction like $\frac{17}{12}$ is called **top heavy**. It can be made into a **mixed number** $1\frac{5}{12}$.

Subtracting fractions

Example: Subtract $\frac{5}{9} - \frac{1}{6}$

First, find the **lowest common multiple** of the two denominators, 9 and 6. The lowest common multiple is the smallest number in the 9 and 6 times table. This is 18.

Now make both fractions into eighteenths.

$\frac{5}{9} = \frac{10}{18}$ (Multiply top and bottom by 2)

$\frac{1}{6} = \frac{3}{18}$ (Multiply top and bottom by 3)

Then just subtract the numerators and leave the denominator unchanged.

$$\frac{5}{9} - \frac{1}{6} = \frac{10}{18} - \frac{3}{18} = \frac{7}{18}$$

Top Tip!

Subtracting a fraction from 1 is a common question e.g. $1 - \frac{11}{14} = \frac{3}{14}$

Write the fraction $\frac{4}{12}$ in its simplest form.

The common factor is 4, so divide top and bottom by 4 to get the answer of $\frac{1}{3}$.

Add a half and a quarter.

The fractions will be really easy, so you should know that

$\frac{1}{2} + \frac{1}{4} = \frac{3}{4}$

level
5

Sample National **Test question**

A vegetable plot is planted with beans, peas, cabbages and carrots.

The peas take up $\frac{1}{4}$ of the plot.

The beans take up $\frac{3}{8}$ of the plot.

The cabbages take up $\frac{1}{6}$ of the plot.

How much of the plot is planted with carrots?

Answer
The total planted with peas, beans and cabbages is:

$\frac{1}{4} + \frac{3}{8} + \frac{1}{6}$

The common denominator is 24.

Making all the fractions into fractions with a denominator of 24 gives:

$\frac{6}{24} + \frac{9}{24} + \frac{4}{24} = \frac{19}{24}$

So $1 - \frac{19}{24} = \frac{5}{24}$ is planted with carrots.

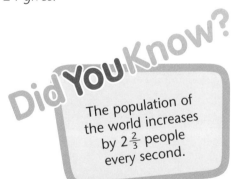

Did You Know?

The population of the world increases by $2\frac{2}{3}$ people every second.

Spot Check

1 Cancel the following fractions to their simplest forms.
   a $\frac{15}{18}$ **b** $\frac{24}{28}$

2 Work out   **a** $\frac{3}{5} + \frac{1}{4}$ **b** $\frac{3}{4} - \frac{1}{6}$

Multiplying fractions

- Adding and subtracting fractions requires denominators to be the same but multiplying and dividing fractions is more straightforward.

Example: Multiply $\frac{2}{3} \times \frac{1}{4}$

When multiplying fractions, the new numerator is the product of the numerators and the new denominator is the product of the denominators.

Multiplying the numerators gives $2 \times 1 = 2$
Multiplying the denominators gives $3 \times 4 = 12$
So $\frac{2}{3} \times \frac{1}{4} = \frac{2}{12}$
This fraction $\frac{2}{12}$ will cancel to $\frac{1}{6}$.

To avoid problems with cancelling, cancel any fractions before multiplying:

$$\frac{\overset{1}{\cancel{2}}}{3} \times \frac{1}{\underset{2}{\cancel{4}}} = \frac{1}{6}$$

In this case, 2 on the top cancels with 4 on the bottom by a common factor of 2.

Example: Multiply $1\frac{1}{4} \times 1\frac{7}{15}$

Write both mixed numbers as **top-heavy** fractions, **cancel common factors** top and bottom and **multiply** the numerators and denominators. Finally, change the top-heavy answer back into a mixed number.

$$\frac{\overset{1}{\cancel{5}}}{\underset{2}{\cancel{4}}} \times \frac{\overset{11}{\cancel{22}}}{\underset{3}{\cancel{15}}} = \frac{11}{6} = 1\frac{5}{6}$$

Top Tip!

Always write mixed numbers as top-heavy fractions when multiplying or dividing.
$3\frac{3}{4} = \frac{15}{4}$ because there are $3 \times 4 = 12$ quarters in 3 plus the extra 3 quarters.

Dividing fractions

- When dividing fractions, turn the **second** fraction **upside down** and **multiply**.

Example: Divide $\frac{5}{6} \div \frac{1}{3}$

Write $\frac{5}{6} \div \frac{1}{3}$ as $\frac{5}{6} \times \frac{3}{1}$

Once again, cancel if you can. In this case, 3 and 6 cancel by a common factor of 3.

$$\frac{5}{\underset{2}{\cancel{6}}} \times \frac{\overset{1}{\cancel{3}}}{1} = \frac{5}{2} = 2\frac{1}{2}$$

Remember to change the top-heavy answer back into a mixed number.

Example: Divide $2\frac{1}{4} \div 1\frac{7}{8}$

Write both mixed numbers as **top-heavy** fractions before turning the **second upside down** and **multiplying**. Then cancel common factors top and bottom and multiply the numerators and denominators. Finally, change the top-heavy answer back into a mixed number.

$$\frac{9}{4} \div \frac{15}{8} = \frac{\overset{3}{\cancel{9}}}{\underset{1}{\cancel{4}}} \times \frac{\overset{2}{\cancel{8}}}{\underset{5}{\cancel{15}}} = \frac{6}{5} = 1\frac{1}{5}$$

Top Tip!

Always cancel before multiplying the numerators and denominators. It makes the calculations much easier.

What is half of one third?

The fractions will be really easy, so you should know that $\frac{1}{2} \times \frac{1}{3} = \frac{1}{6}$

How many fifths are there in 2?

There are 5 fifths in 1, so there are 10 fifths in 2.

Sample National 💡 Test question

Work out $3\frac{3}{4} \div \frac{5}{8}$

Answer

Write the calculation as $\frac{15}{4} \div \frac{5}{8}$

Now turn the second fraction upside down and multiply $\frac{\overset{3}{\cancel{15}}}{\cancel{4}} \times \frac{\overset{2}{\cancel{8}}}{\cancel{5}} = \frac{6}{1}$

Cancel where possible.

The calculation is $3\frac{3}{4} \div \frac{5}{8} = 6$

Top Tip!

Any fraction with a denominator of 1 is a whole number.

Did You Know?

One mile in every five of the US motorway network has to be straight so that it can be used as an airstrip in emergencies.

Spot Check

1 Work out **a** $\frac{5}{8} \times \frac{4}{15}$ **b** $2\frac{2}{3} \times 1\frac{1}{8}$

2 Work out **a** $\frac{2}{9} \div \frac{8}{15}$ **b** $2\frac{4}{5} \div 2\frac{1}{10}$

NUMBER Equivalent fractions, percentages and decimals

Simple fractions and percentages

- You need to be able to recognise some simple fractions and percentages.

Example: In this pie chart **a** what fraction is blue **b** what percentage is red?

Favourite colours

a Half ($\frac{1}{2}$) of the pie is labelled blue.

b A quarter is labelled red, so the percentage is 25%.

> **Top Tip!**
>
> The common percentages you should be able to recognise are:
>
> 25%   50%   75% $33\frac{1}{3}$% $66\frac{2}{3}$%.
>
> These are the same as the fractions:
>
> $\frac{1}{4}$ $\frac{1}{2}$ $\frac{3}{4}$ $\frac{1}{3}$ $\frac{2}{3}$

Fractions, percentages and decimals

- Fractions, percentages and decimals represent the **same value** and you should know the **equivalences** between them.
- You should know the following equivalences:

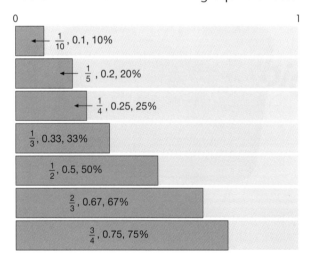

Example: Find the equivalent decimal and fraction to 40%.

$40\% = 2 \times 20\% = 2 \times \frac{1}{5} = \frac{2}{5}$
$= 2 \times 0.2 = 0.4$

> **Top Tip!**
>
> Use the known equivalences such as $10\% = \frac{1}{10} = 0.1$ to work out others such as 5% and 15%.

Example: Find the equivalent decimal and percentage to $\frac{4}{25}$.

$\frac{4}{25} = \frac{16}{100} = 16\%$
$16\% = 0.16$

> **Top Tip!**
>
> The decimal equivalent to a percentage is the percentage divided by 100.

Sample mental  test question

What percentage is equivalent to the decimal 0.35?

As this is a mental question, you should be able to split the calculation:
0.35 = 3 x 0.1 + 0.05 = 30% + 5% = 35%.

level
5

Sample National Test question

The pie charts show the ages of people in a village and a town.

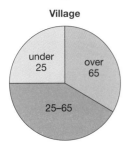

Village

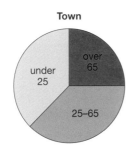

Town

a What percentage of the village are over 65?

b What percentage of the town are over 65?

c Tick the box that is true.

☐ There are more people over 65 in the village than the town.

☐ There are fewer people over 65 in the village than the town.

☐ There are equal numbers of people over 65 in the village and the town.

☐ You cannot tell how many people over 65 there are in the village and the town.

Explain your answer.

Answers

a 33% of the village are over 65.

b 25% of the town are over 65.

*c You cannot tell how many people are over 65 because the pie chart only shows the **proportions** and not the **actual numbers**. There may be more people in the town so 25% of a larger population may be more than 33% of a smaller population.*

Top Tip!

National Test questions often test if you understand that pie charts only show proportions and not actual values.

Did You Know?

90% of people think that the American Thomas Edison invented the lightbulb. This isn't true. It was invented by Joseph Swan in Newcastle, England.

Spot Check

1 Fill in the missing equivalences in the table.

Decimal	Percentage	Fraction
0.15	15%	3/20
0.35	35%	35/100 7/20
0.9	90%	9/10

NUMBER   Percentages

level
5

Percentage parts

- You should know that per cent means 'out of a hundred'.

Example: Work out **a** 15% of £45   **b** 32% of 75 kg

     a 10% of £45 is £4.50, so 5% of £45 is £2.25
        15% of £45 is £4.50 + £2.25 = £6.75

     b On the calculator, do 32 ÷ 100 x 75 = 24 kg
        or 0.32 x 75 = 24 kg.

Top Tip!

On the non-calculator paper, Paper 1, the percentage will always be a multiple of 5 or 10.

level
5

Percentage increases and decreases

Example: A car's top speed is 125 mph. After a tune-up, its top speed increases by 12%. What is the new top speed?

Method 1

Work out 12% of 125.

12 ÷ 100 x 125 = 15

Add this to the original speed: 125 + 15 = 140 mph

Method 2

Use a **multiplier**. A 12% increase is a multiplier of 1.12.

1.12 x 125 = 140 mph

Top Tip!

Think of the **per cent** sign as '÷ 100' and the '**of**' as a **times** sign. So 43% of 150 is 43 ÷ 100 x 150 = 64.5.

Top Tip!

Calculations are much easier if a 'multiplier' is used.
32% is a multiplier of 0.32.
An increase of 15% is a multiplier of 1.15.
A decrease of 8% is a multiplier of 0.92.
Percentages are easily converted to decimals. Just divide by 100 (or move digits).

level
6

One quantity as a percentage of another

Example: What percentage is 42 out of 56?

The fraction is $\frac{42}{56}$.
This is divided to give the decimal: 42 ÷ 56 = 0.75.
This decimal is multiplied by 100 to give the percentage.
The whole calculation can be done as
42 ÷ 56 x 100 = 75%.

Top Tip!

If you divide the numerator by the denominator this gives the percentage multiplier:
42 ÷ 56 = 0.75, which is 75%.

Example: 17 students in a class of 25 stay for school dinners. What percentage is this?

The fraction is $\frac{17}{25}$.
Multiply the **numerator** (top number) by 4 and multiply the **denominator** (bottom number) by 4.

$$\frac{17 \times 4}{25 \times 4} = \frac{68}{100}$$

So the answer is 68%.

What is 20% of £30?

Start by calculating 10%, which is £3, and then double it to £6.

In a test I got 16 out of 20. What percentage did I get?

Convert the denominator to 10 or 100.

16 out of 20 is the same as 8 out of 10, which is 80%.

level
5

Sample National Test question

30 students were asked how they travelled to school.

Transport	Boys	Girls
Walk	2	6
Bus	1	9
Car	2	7
Cycle	0	3
Total	5	25

a What percentage of boys come by bus?

b What percentage of girls walk to school?

c Misha said, 'Girls are healthier than boys because more of them walk to school'. Explain why she was wrong.

Answers

a 1 out of 5 is 20%.

b 6 out of 25 is $\frac{6}{25} = \frac{24}{100} = 24\%$.

c *Although more girls walk than boys (6 compared to 2), the percentages are $\frac{2}{5} = 40\%$ for boys, and $\frac{6}{25} = 24\%$ for girls.*

Top Tip!

Make the denominator into 100 by multiplying by a factor of 100 and do the same thing to the numerator.
Learn the factors of 100:

1 x 100

2 x 50

4 x 25

5 x 20

10 x 10

Did You Know?

In 1971 80% of 8 year olds walked to school. In 2001 the figure was just 7%.

Spot Check

1 Work out **a** £75 increased by 20%

b 120 kg decreased by 12%

NUMBER Ratio

level 5

Ratio

- Ratio is a way of **comparing quantities**.
  For example, if there are 18 girls and 12 boys in a class, the ratio is 18 : 12.
  Because 18 and 12 have a **common factor** of 6, this can be cancelled down to 3 : 2.
  This is called the **simplest form**.

Example: Reduce the ratio 15 : 25 to its simplest form.
  The highest common factor of 15 and 25 is 5.
  Cancelling (dividing) both numbers by 5 gives 3 : 5.

- You may also be asked **direct proportion** questions.

Example: If 6 pencils cost £1.32, how much will 10 pencils cost?

  Using **ratio**:
  6 : 132 cancels to 1 : 22
  Multiplying by 10 gives 10 : 220, so 10 pencils will cost £2.20.

  Using the **unitary method**:
  If 6 pencils cost £1.32, 1 pencil costs 1.32 ÷ 6 = £0.22
  So 10 pencils cost 10 x £0.22 = £2.20.

  These two methods are basically the same.

> **Top Tip!**
> Use whichever method is easiest for the question. The unitary method is easier for this example because 6 : 132 is not an easy ratio to cancel

level 6

Calculating with ratio

- You need to be able to carry out different calculations involving ratios.

Example: If a family of 3 and a family of 2 had a meal and decided to split the bill of £35 between the two families, how much should each family pay?

  It wouldn't be fair to split the bill in two, as there are more people in one of the families.
  The bill should be split in the ratio 2 : 3.
  The ratio 2 : 3 is a total of 2 + 3 = 5 shares.
  Each share will be 35 ÷ 5 = 7.
  2 x 7 = 14 and 3 x 7 = 21, so the £35 should be split as £14 and £21.

> **Top Tip!**
> Always check that the final ratios or values add up to the value you started with, e.g. 14 + 21 = 35.

Spot Check
1 Write the ratio 14 : 18 in its simplest form.
2 Share £32 in the ratio 3 : 5.

Sample mental test questions

Look at the ratio 4 : 10. Write it in its simplest form.

The numbers will make finding a common factor easy.

In this case they cancel by 2 to give 2 : 5.

Divide £100 in the ratio 3 : 7.

The numbers will be easy to divide.

3 + 7 = 10, 100 ÷ 10 = 10, so the shares are £30 and £70.

level
6

Sample National Test question

Aunt Vera decides to give her nephews, Arnie, Barney and Clyde, £180.
The money is to be divided in the ratio of their ages.

Arnie is 1, Barney is 2 and Clyde is 3.

a   How much do they each receive?

b   The next year she decides to share another £180
between the three boys in the ratio of their ages.
How much do they each receive the following year?

Answers

a   *The total of their ages is 6, so divide 180 by 6.*

180 ÷ 6 = 30

Arnie gets 1 x 30 = £30.

Barney gets 2 x 30 = £60.

Clyde gets 3 x 30 = £90.

Don't forget to check the totals:
30 + 60 + 90 = £180

b   *The following year the ages are 2, 3 and 4. This is a total of 9.*

180 ÷ 9 = 20

Arnie gets 2 x 20 = £40.

Barney gets 3 x 20 = £60.

Clyde gets 4 x 20 = £80.

Did You Know?

The 'Golden ratio', is about 1.618.
Leonardo Da Vinci used the
proportions of the Golden ratio in
the painting of the Mona Lisa.

Term-to-term rule

- A number pattern is a **sequence** or series of numbers that follow a **rule**.
- You should be able to say what the next two terms in this sequence are:

  3, 7, 11, 15, 19, ... , ...

  First look for the rule.

  In this case each number is 4 more than the previous number.

  This is called the **term-to-term rule**.

  So the next two numbers are 19 + 4 = 23 and 23 + 4 = 27.

- Sometimes the term-to-term rule is not so straightforward.

Example: Find the next two terms in this series of numbers and describe how the series is developed: 1, 3, 6, 10, 15, ... , ...

The next two terms are 21 and 28.

The series is built up by adding on 2, 3, 4, etc.

- The series 1, 3, 6, 10, 15, ... is a special series called the **triangle numbers** because the numbers can be made into triangle patterns.

> **Top Tip!**
>
> If you are asked to describe how a pattern builds up, say 'It goes up by 4 each time'.

> **Top Tip!**
>
> A good way of remembering the triangle numbers is to think of snooker and ten-pin bowling. Snooker has 15 red balls in a triangle and ten-pin bowling has 10 pins in a triangle.

The nth term of a sequence

- Sequences can also be described using algebraic rules.

Example: The nth term of a sequence is given by $2n - 1$.

Write down the first five terms of the sequence.

Substitute $n = 1, 2, 3, 4$ and 5 into the rule.

$n = 1$ gives $2 \times 1 - 1 = 1$

$n = 2$ gives $2 \times 2 - 1 = 3$

$n = 3$ gives $2 \times 3 - 1 = 5$

$n = 4$ gives $2 \times 4 - 1 = 7$

$n = 5$ gives $2 \times 5 - 1 = 9$

So the sequence is: 1, 3, 5, 7, 9, ... which are the odd numbers.

> **Top Tip!**
>
> The nth term is useful for finding out a number in a sequence without writing out all the sequence.

- There is a quick way of finding out the nth term.

Example: Find the nth term of the sequence: 4, 9, 14, 19, 24, 29, ...

What does each term go up by? In this case, 5.

The nth term will start $5n$.

What do you do to go from 5 to the first number, 4?

In this case, minus 1.

The nth term will be $5n$ minus 1 or $5n - 1$.

Example: Find the nth term of the sequence: 4, 7, 10, 13, 16, ...

The terms increase in steps of 3.

$3 + 1 = 4$, so the nth term is $3n + 1$.

Sample mental test questions

I start at 5 and count down in equal steps: 5, 2, –1. What is the next number in the sequence?

First decide on the step. In this case, it is subtract 3.

Minus 1 subtract 3 is minus 4, so the answer is –4.

The nth term of a sequence is $(n + 2)^2$.

What is the 4th term of the sequence?

Substitute 4 for n:

$(4 + 2)^2 = 6^2 = 36$

Sample National Test question

The following patterns are made up of black and white hexagons.

Pattern 1   Pattern 2   Pattern 3   Pattern 4

Complete this table.

Pattern	Black hexagons	White hexagons
5		
10		
n		

Answers

The fifth pattern has 5 black hexagons and 11 white hexagons. You should realise that the number of black hexagons is the same as the pattern number and the number of white hexagons is double the pattern number plus 1.

So the table is:

Pattern	Black hexagons	White hexagons
5	*5*	*11*
10	*10*	*21*
n	*n*	*$2n + 1$*

Top Tip!

Write out the sequence of numbers as a list. This will help you to see the nth term:

Black hexagons: 1 2 3 4 5

So the nth term is n.

White hexagons: 3 5 7 9 11

So the nth term is $2n + 1$.

Did You Know?

The Fibonacci sequence 1, 1, 2, 3, 5, 8, 13 … is where each term is formed by the sum of the two preceding numbers. This sequence can be found in nature, for example, in seed heads, flower petals and sea shells.

Spot Check

1 What is the next term in the sequence: 3, 7, 11, 15, 19, …

2 What is the nth term of the sequence: 4, 8, 12, 16, 20, …

3 What is the nth term of the sequence: 5, 9, 13, 17, 21, …

ALGEBRA · Multiples, factors, square numbers and primes

Multiples and factors

- The **multiples** of a number are its **times table**. The **factors** of a number are the numbers that **divide exactly** into it. 1 and the number itself are always factors.

Example: Write down the first five multiples of 15.

The first five numbers in the 15 times table are:

15, 30, 45, 60, 75, ...

Example: Find the factors of 24.

Look for all the products of whole numbers that make 24:

1 x 24, 2 x 12, 3 x 8, 4 x 6

The factors of 24 are: {1, 2, 3, 4, 6, 8, 12, 24}

> **Top Tip!**
> Factors come in pairs except for square numbers, where one number is its own 'pair':
> 2 x 2, 3 x 3, 4 x 4.

Square numbers

Example: Find the next two numbers in this series and describe how the series is built up:

1, 4, 9, 16, 25, ... , ...

The next two terms are 36 and 49.

The series is built up by adding on 3, 5, 7, 9, 11, and so on.

- Another way of spotting this series is to realise that each number can be written as: 1 x 1, 2 x 2, 3 x 3, 4 x 4, 5 x 5.

These numbers can be written using a special symbol called **square** or the **power 2** as: $1^2, 2^2, 3^2, 4^2, 5^2$.

> **Top Tip!**
> 3^2 is spoken as 'three squared'.

> **Top Tip!**
> The series 1, 4, 9, 16, 25, ... is a special series called the **square numbers** because the numbers can be made into square patterns:

Square roots

- The opposite of square is **square root** which is shown by the symbol $\sqrt{81}$.

Example: **a** Find $\sqrt{81}$ **b** The value of x if $x^2 = 36$

a $\sqrt{81} = 9$ because 9 x 9 = 81

b $x = 6$ or -6 because 6 x 6 = 36 and -6 x -6 = 36

> **Top Tip!**
> Square roots are usually taken as positive but the solution to $x^2 = 36$ has two possible answers: ±6 (plus or minus 6).

Prime numbers

• Numbers that only have two factors (1 and itself) are called **prime numbers**.

There is no pattern to the prime numbers, you just have to learn them or work them out. The prime numbers up to 50 are:

2, 3, 5, 7, 11, 13, 17, 19, 23, 29, 31, 37, 41, 43, 47

Top Tip!

2 is the only even prime number. National Test questions often test if you know this.

Sample mental test question

x squared is 36. What are the possible values of $2 + x$?

First, x must be +6 or –6, so $2 + 6 = 8$ and $2 + –6 = –4$
So there are two answers: 8 and –4.

levels
4-5

Sample National Test questions

a Circle the numbers below that are factors of 60.
5   10   15   20   25   30
35   40   45   50   55   60

b Solve the equation
$x^2 – 4 = 60$

c From the list below write down:
i a square number   **ii** a multiple of 7   **iii** a prime number
13   15   17   19   21   23
25   27   29   31   33   35

Answers
a *The numbers that divide into 60 are 5, 10, 15, 20, 30 and 60.*
b *x^2 must equal 64, so $x = 8$ or –8.*
c **i** *The only square number in the list is 25.*
ii *There are two multiples of 7 in the list: 21 and 35.*
iii *There are several prime numbers in the list. Choose any from 13, 17, 19, 23, 29 or 31.*

Did You Know? Each square centimetre of your skin has about 100 000 bacteria on it.

Spot Check

1 From the list below write down:
a a square number   **b** a prime number
c a multiple of 4   **d** a multiple of 3 and 7
3   6   9   12   15   18   21

ALGEBRA — Basic algebra

Simplifying expressions

- **Algebra** uses **letters** to **represent values** in equations, expressions and identities. You need to be able to simplify and manipulate algebraic expressions.

Example: Simplify **a** $2a + 3a$ **b** $3 \times 4a$ **c** $4a \times 5b$ **d** $2a \times 3a$
e $3a + 5b + 4a - 3b$ **f** $6a + 4 + 2a + 3$

a $2a + 3a = 5a$
b $3 \times 4a = 12a$
c $4a \times 5b = 20ab$
d $2a \times 3a = 6a^2$
e $3a + 5b + 4a - 3b = 7a + 2b$
f $6a + 4 + 2a + 3 = 8a + 7$

> **Top Tip!**
> $3a = 3 \times a$
> The 'x' sign is assumed between a number and a letter.
> Also $\frac{a}{3} = a \div 3$

Substituting numbers

- You need to be able to substitute numbers into expressions to find a value.

Example: If $a = 3$, $b = 4$ and $c = 7$, find the value of:
a $a + b$ **b** $2a$ **c** $4c - 5$ **d** $a^2 + b^2$ **e** $a(b + c)$

a $a + b = 3 + 4 = 7$
b $2a = 2 \times 3 = 6$
c $4c - 5 = 4 \times 7 - 5 = 23$
d $a^2 + b^2 = 3^2 + 4^2 = 3 \times 3 + 4 \times 4 = 25$
e $a(b + c) = 3(4 + 7) = 3 \times 11 = 33$

> **Top Tip!**
> Replace the letters by the numbers before doing the calculation.
> Don't try to do it in your head:
> If $a = 2$, $b = 6$,
> $a + b = 2 + 6 = 8$
> $2a = 2 \times 2 = 4$
> $b^2 = 6^2 = 36$

Interpreting expressions

- You need to be able to interpret expressions.

Example: Imran is x years old. His sister Aisha is 3 years older. His brother Mushtaq is twice as old as Imran.

    a How old is Aisha?
    b How old is Mushtaq?
    c What is the total of their three ages?

> **Top Tip!**
> You cannot add together terms that contain different letters.
> You cannot simplify $8a + 2b$.

    a Aisha is 3 years older than Imran so she is $x + 3$ years old.
    b Mushtaq is twice as old as Imran so he is $2x$ years old.
    c The total is $x + x + 3 + 2x = 4x + 3$ years.

Sample mental test question

Look at the expression $2a + 5b + 6a - b$ and simplify it.

Combine the terms containing a, and then the terms containing b.
The answer is $8a + 4b$.

level
4-5

Sample National Test question

There are n students in Form 9A.

a These expressions show how many students are in Forms 9A and 9B.
Write the number of students in 9C in words.

| 9A | n | students |
| 9B | $n + 2$ | students | 2 more students than 9A |

| 9A | n | students |
| 9C | $n - 3$ | students | .... |

b Two students move from Form 9A to Form 9B.
Write down the number of students in Forms 9A and 9B now.
9A has .... students. 9B has .... students.

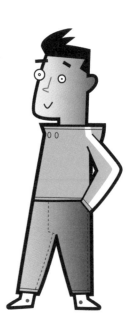

Answers
a *9C has 3 fewer students than 9A.*
b *Taking 2 from n gives $n - 2$ and adding 2 to $n + 2$ gives $n + 4$.*
9A has $n - 2$ students. 9B has $n + 4$ students.

Did You Know?

On August 21, 1965, Charlton Athletic's Keith Peacock became the first substitute to appear in the Football League.

Spot Check

1 Simplify **a** $4a + 3 - 2a + 1$ **b** $4b \times 5b$

2 If $x = 3$ and $y = 4$, work out **a** $4x + 5y$ **b** $x^2 + y^2$

ALGEBRA   Formulae

Formulae in words

- A **formula** is a rule that changes one number into another.

Example: **a** How much would it cost to park for 4 hours?

b If the total is £2, for how many hours was the car parked?

CAR PARK
£1 plus 50p per hour

a To park for 4 hours would cost £1 + 4 x £0.50 = £3.

b If it cost £2 to park, the car was there for 2 hours.

In this case the rule changes the number of hours parking (the input) into the cost of parking (output).

Flow diagrams

Example: Look at the flow diagram below.

a If the input is 6 what is the output?   **b** What is the input if the output is 21?

INPUT → Multiply by 2 → Add 3 → OUTPUT

> **Top Tip!**
> A flow diagram can be used to help solve equations:
> $$2x + 3 = 21$$
> $$x = 9$$
> 9 → ×2 → +3 → 21

a An input of 6 gives an output of 6 x 2 + 3 = 15.

b To find an input from an output **work backwards** through the flow diagram.

An output of 21 has an input of (21 − 3) ÷ 2 = 9.

Example: To cook a turkey, use this formula:

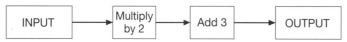

Cooking time (in min) = Weight of turkey (in kg) x 30 min + 30 min

a How long will it take to cook a 6 kilogram turkey?

b If a turkey took 5 hours to cook, how much did it weigh?

a Cooking time = 6 x 30 min plus 30 min

= 210 min = 3 hours and 30 min

b 5 hours = 300 min

Deduct 30 min: 300 − 30 = 270 min

Divide by 30: 270 ÷ 30 = 9

The turkey weighed 9 kilograms.

> **Top Tip!**
> Try to write the rule in symbols:
> $T = W \times 30 + 30$
> So, if $W = 6$,
> $T = 6 \times 30 + 30 = 210$

Look at the flow diagram. What is the input if the output is 7?

Input → x 2 → − 1 → Output

*You should know to work **backwards** through the flow diagram: 7 + 1 = 8, 8 ÷ 2 = 4.*
The input is 4.

levels
4-5

Sample National ♀ Test question

The following rule can be used to predict the height of a boy when he is an adult.

Add 20 cm to the father's height (in cm).
Add the mother's height (in cm).
Divide by 2.
The boy's height will be within 10 cm of this height.

What will be the range of the adult height of a boy whose father is 174 cm tall and whose mother is 158 cm tall?

Answer
Add 20 cm to father's height: 174 + 20 = 194
Add the mother's height: 194 + 158 = 352
Divide by 2: 352 ÷ 2 = 176 cm
The boy's height will be between 166 cm and 186 cm.

Did You Know?

Toothpaste was first sold commercially in 1873 but the earliest formula for toothpaste was written in the fourth century. (It contained soot!)

Spot Check

1 I think of a number, multiply it by 3 and subtract 4. The result is 17. What was the number I thought of?

2 Input → ÷ 4 → + 2 → Output

What is the output if the input is 16?

Coordinates in the first quadrant

• **Coordinates** are used to describe the **position** of a point on a grid.

Example: A, B and C are three sides of a square.

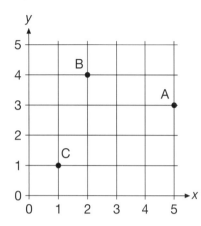

a Write down the coordinates of A, B and C.
b On the grid, plot D, the fourth corner of the square.

a A is (5, 3), B is (2, 4) and C is (1, 1).
b D should be plotted at the point (4, 0).

Top Tip!
There are two rules to remember. Start at the **origin** (0, 0) and move **horizontally** first, then **vertically** second.

Coordinates in all four quadrants

• **Negative coordinates** can also be used to describe the position of a point on a grid.

Example: A, B and C are three sides of a square.

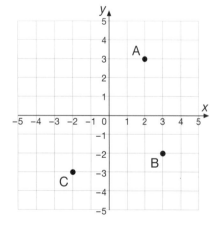

a Write down the coordinates of A, B and C.
b On the grid, plot D, the fourth corner of the square.

a A is (2, 3), B is (3, −2) and C is (−2, −3).
b D should be plotted at the point (−3, 2).

Top Tip!
Read the value from the *x*-axis first, and the value from the *y*-axis second.

The point P is (−2, −3).

Look at the grid.

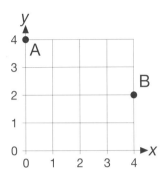

What are the coordinates of the midpoint AB?

The midpoint is (2, 3).

The graph shows the line $y = 2x$.

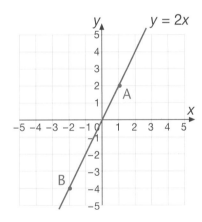

a   Write down the coordinates of the points A and B.

b   The point C (–8, –16) is on the line.
Explain how you know this is true.

Answers

a   A is (1, 2) and B is (–2, –4)

b   The y-value is twice the x-value.

$$2 \times -8 = -16$$

Did You Know?

All Ordnance Survey maps are based on a coordinate grid. The origin is a point to the south-west of the Isles of Scilly.

pot Check

1   A is the point (6, –2) and B is the point (4, –2). What are the coordinates of the point halfway between A and B?

2   Which axis should you always read first?

Drawing graphs

Drawing graphs by plotting points

- Graphs show the relationship between variables on a coordinate grid.

  For example, the equation $y = 2x + 1$ shows a relationship between x and y where the y-value is 2 times the x-value plus 1.

  If $x = 0$, $y = 2 \times 0 + 1 = 1$. This can be represented by the coordinates (0, 1).

- Similarly, when $x = 1$, $y = 2 \times 1 + 1 = 3$. This is the point (1, 3).

  Other coordinates connecting x and y are (–3, –5), (–1, –1), (2, 5), etc.

  When these are plotted on a graph, they can be joined by a straight line.

- Coordinates are always given in the order: (x, y).

Example: Draw the graph of $y = 3x - 1$.
First find some points by choosing x-values:
Let $x = 0$, $y = 3 \times 0 - 1 = -1$
Let $x = 1$, $y = 3 \times 1 - 1 = 2$
Let $x = 2$, $y = 3 \times 2 - 1 = 5$
Let $x = -1$, $y = 3 \times -1 - 1 = -4$
Plot the points and join them up.

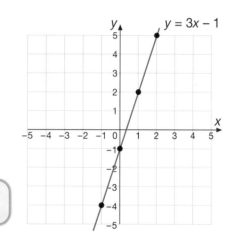

Top Tip!

Always label graphs.

Drawing graphs by the gradient intercept method

- In an equation like $y = mx + c$, c is where the graph crosses the y-axis and m is the gradient.

  So for $y = 3x - 1$, the graph crosses the y-axis at –1 and has a gradient of 3. This means for every 1 unit across, the graph goes up by 3 units.

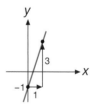

Example: Draw the graph of $y = 2x - 1$.
Start by plotting the point (0, –1).
Then from (0, –1) count 1 square across and 2 squares up, mark a point, repeat from this point and so on. You can also count 1 square back and 2 squares down.

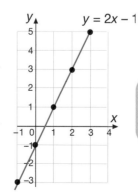

Top Tip!

Remember to read the x-axis first then the y-axis.

Sample mental test question

Look at the equation $y = 3x + 2$.

What is the value of y when $x = 2$?

Substitute $x = 2$ into the equation, so $y = 3 \times 2 + 2 = 8$

Sample National Test question

A is the point (2, 4).

B is the point (−4, −2).

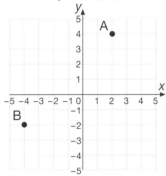

Which of the following equations is the graph of the straight line through A and B?

$y = 2x \qquad y = x + 2 \qquad y = -2x \qquad y = \dfrac{x}{2}$

Explain your answer.

Top Tip!

Substitute the x- and y-values into the equations for all the pairs of coordinates you are given.

Answer

The equation is $y = x + 2$. This is the only equation that fits both A and B.

For A: $4 = 2 + 2$

For B: $-2 = -4 + 2$

Did You Know?

Nobody knows why x and y are used as the main letters in algebra, but x is now taken to represent something 'unknown', e.g. the X-files!

pot Check

1 Complete the table for $y = 3x - 2$ for values of x from −2 to +4.

x	−2	−1	0	1	2	3	4
y	−8						10

Linear graphs

x and y lines

- There are some graphs that you need to learn.

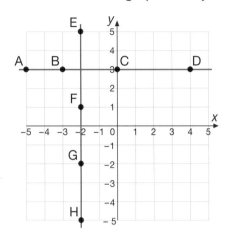

Top Tip!

All lines of the form $y = b$ are horizontal, and lines of the form $x = a$ are vertical.

Top Tip!

The x-axis is the line $y = 0$.
The y-axis is the line $x = 0$.

- The coordinates of the points A, B, C and D are (–5, 3), (–3, 3), (0, 3), (4, 3) respectively.

  You can see that they all have a y-coordinate of 3 and form a straight line on the grid.

  This line has an equation $y = 3$.

- The coordinates of the points E, F, G and H on the graph above are (–2, 5), (–2, 1), (–2, –2), (–2, –5) respectively.

  You can see that they all have an x-coordinate of –2 and form a straight line on the grid.

  This line has an equation $x = –2$.

x and y graphs

- Two other graphs that you need to know are:

$$y = x \qquad\qquad y = -x$$

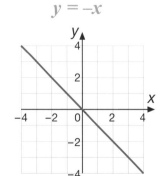

$x + y = c$ graphs

- The coordinates of the points A, B, C and D are (–3, 5), (0, 2), (3, –1), (5, –3) respectively.

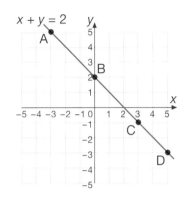

You can see that the x- and y-coordinates add up to a total of 2. This line has an equation $x + y = 2$.

Top Tip!

All lines of the form $x + y = c$ slope at 45° from top left to bottom right, and pass through the value c on both axes.

Sample National Test question

The graph shows a triangle.

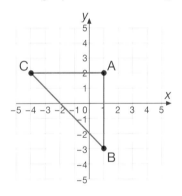

a What is the equation of the line through A and B?
b What is the equation of the line through A and C?
c What is the equation of the line through B and C?

Answers

a $x = 1$. AB is a vertical line through 1 on the x-axis.
b $y = 2$. AC is a horizontal line through 2 on the y-axis.
c $x + y = -2$. The line passes through (0, –2) and (–2, 0).

Did You Know?

René Descartes devised x- and y-coordinates in the seventeenth century. The grid is also called the Cartesian plane after Descartes.

Spot Check

1 Give the equations of the lines A, B and C.

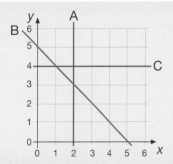

Order of operations

• To calculate 2 + 3 x 4, work out 3 x 4 first and then add this to 2 to give 14.
  This calculation uses the rules of mathematical operations, which is known as **BODMAS**.

• **BODMAS** stands for **B**rackets, **O**rder, **D**ivision, **M**ultiplication, **A**ddition, **S**ubtraction.
  This is the order in which operations must be done.
  For example:
  Brackets are always worked out first.
  Powers are always worked out before multiplication.

> **Top Tip!**
> **Order** is another name for **power**. In the National Tests, the powers will be **square** (power 2) or **cube** (power 3).

Example: Work out **a** $10 - 2 \times 3$ **b** $(10 - 2) \times 3$

      a According to BODMAS, multiplication comes
      before subtraction, so find 2 x 3 first.
      The calculation is: $10 - 2 \times 3 = 10 - 6 = 4$.

      b BODMAS tells you to work out the bracket first.
      The calculation is: $(10 - 2) \times 3 = 8 \times 3 = 24$.

Example: Work out **a** $20 \div 4^2$ **b** $(20 \div 4)^2$

      a BODMAS tells you to work out the power (order) first, and then do the division.
      The calculation is: $20 \div 4^2 = 20 \div 16 = 1.25$ or $1\frac{1}{4}$.

      b BODMAS tells you to work out the bracket first, and then find the power.
      The calculation is: $(20 \div 4)^2 = 5^2 = 25$.

Example: Put brackets in the following calculations to make them true:

      a $3 + 4 \times 5 - 1 = 28$ **b** $3 + 2^2 + 6 = 31$

      a As the calculation is written it works out as $3 + 4 \times 5 - 1 = 3 + 20 - 1 = 22$.
      By trying out brackets we can see that $(3 + 4) \times (5 - 1) = 7 \times 4 = 28$.

      b As the calculation is written it works out as $3 + 2^2 + 6 = 3 + 4 + 6 = 13$.
      By trying out brackets we can see that $(3 + 2)^2 + 6 = 5^2 + 6 = 25 + 6 = 31$.

levels
4-5

Powers

• You have already met the powers 2 (square) and 3 (cube). Powers are a short way of writing repeated multiplications so $3^4 = 3 \times 3 \times 3 \times 3 = 81$, $2^5 = 2 \times 2 \times 2 \times 2 \times 2 = 32$.

Example: Which is greater 3^5 or 5^3?
      $3^5 = 3 \times 3 \times 3 \times 3 \times 3 = 243$, $5^3 = 5 \times 5 \times 5 = 125$
      So 3^5 is greater.

> **Top Tip!**
> You should know the squares of all the numbers up to 15^2 and the cubes of 1, 2, 3, 4, 5, and 10.

Look at the expression $3m^2$.

What is the value of the expression when $m = 10$?

Using BODMAS, $3m^2 = 3 \times m^2 = 3 \times 10^2 = 3 \times 100 = 300$.

level
5

Sample National Test questions

a Write the answers to:

   i $(5 + 3) \times 4$ **ii** $5 + (3 \times 4)$

b Work out the answer to: $(8 - 3) \times (4^2 \div 2)$

c **i** Put brackets in the calculation to make the answer correct:

   $16 \div 2 + 6 \times 4 = 8$

   ii Put brackets in the calculation to make the answer correct:

   $16 \div 2 + 6 \times 4 = 56$

Answers

a *Using the rules of BODMAS the answers are:*

   i $8 \times 4 = 32$ ii $5 + 12 = 17$

b *Work out the brackets first. Within the second bracket, the power should be calculated first.*

   $(8 - 3) \times (4^2 \div 2) = 5 \times (16 \div 2) = 5 \times 8 = 40$

c *Trying brackets in various places gives:*

   i $16 \div (2 + 6) \times 4 = 16 \div 8 \times 4 = 2 \times 4 = 8$

   ii $(16 \div 2 + 6) \times 4 = (8 + 6) \times 4 = 14 \times 4 = 56$

Did You Know?

The only two words with the vowels used once and in order are 'abstemious' and 'facetious'.

Spot Check

1 Work out **a** $5 + 5^2 \div 10$ **b** $(5 + 5)^2 \div 10$

2 Put brackets in this calculation to make it true: $9 + 6 \div 3 + 5 = 10$

ALGEBRA   Equations 1

Basic equations

- 'I am thinking of a number. I double it and add 6. The answer is 12. What was the number I thought of?'

  This type of question can usually be solved in your head to give the answer 3.

- It can also be written as an **equation**.

  An equation is an expression involving a certain letter, x say, that is equal to a number.

  '**Solving the equation**' means **finding** the **value** of x that makes it true.

Example: The puzzle above could be written as: $2x + 6 = 12$

To solve this equation, you need x on its own on the left-hand side of the equals sign. You do this by applying the **inverse operations** to **both sides**.

First, eliminate '+ 6' by doing the inverse operation '– 6':

$2x = 6$

Now eliminate 'x 2' by doing the inverse operation '÷ 2':

$x = 3$

Example: Solve **a** $\frac{x}{2} - 3 = 7$ **b** $\frac{x-3}{2} = 6$

a First add 3, then multiply by 2.

$\frac{x}{2} = 10$

$x = 20$

b First multiply by 2 and then add 3.

$x - 3 = 12$

$x = 15$

> **Top Tip!**
>
> There are different ways of writing the solution to an equation, but they all arrive at the same solution:
>
> $2x + 6 - 6 = 12 - 6$
>
> $2x = 6$
>
> $2x \div 2 = 6 \div 2$
>
> $x = 3$

Fractional equations

- A **fractional equation** is one in which the **variable** appears as the numerator or **denominator** of a fraction.

Example: Solve the equation $\frac{x}{2} = \frac{7}{4}$

The first step in solving a fractional equation is to **cross-multiply**. This means multiply the denominator of the left-hand side by the numerator of the right-hand side and multiply the denominator of the right-hand side by the numerator of the left-hand side.

So: $4 \times x = 2 \times 7$

Tidy up the terms: $4x = 14$

Solve the equation: $x = 3\frac{1}{2}$ or 3.5

> **Top Tip!**
>
> You could just write down $4x = 14$ and then solve the equation. Answers can be left as top-heavy fractions, such as $\frac{14}{4} = \frac{7}{2}$ unless you are asked for an answer in its **simplest form**.

Example: Solve the equation $\frac{2}{x} = \frac{7}{11}$

Cross-multiplying: $22 = 7x$

This equation has the x-term on the right so reverse the equation: $7x = 22$

Divide by 7: $x = \frac{22}{7} = 3\frac{1}{7}$

> **Top Tip!**
>
> You can remember cross-multiplying by thinking of
>
> $\frac{x}{2} \bowtie \frac{7}{4}$
>
> which is where the term 'cross' comes from.

Look at the equation $3x - 4 = 11$.

What value of x makes the equation true?

If $3x - 4 = 11$, $3x = 15$ and $x = 5$.

Sample National Test question

Solve the equations to find the values of x, y and z.

$$3x + 10$$
$$\frac{y}{2} - 10 \longrightarrow = 40$$
$$z^2 + 4$$

Answers

$3x + 10 = 40 \Rightarrow 3x = 30 \Rightarrow x = 10$

$\frac{y}{2} - 10 = 40 \Rightarrow \frac{y}{2} = 50 \Rightarrow y = 100$

$z^2 + 4 = 40 \Rightarrow z^2 = 36 \Rightarrow z = 6$ *(or -6)*

Did You Know?

The world's largest jigsaw puzzle had 18240 pieces and took 10 months to solve.

 **Spot Check**

1 Solve the equations   **a** $3x - 8 = 10$ **b** $\frac{x}{4} = \frac{5}{2}$

2 Look at these cards.

$2x - 5$	$5x + 9$	$3x + 7$	$4x + 1$
Card A	Card B	Card C	Card D

a What value of x makes card A equal to 8?

b What value of x makes card B equal to 4?

c What value of x makes card C equal to 7?

d What value of x makes card D equal to 0?

Equations with brackets

- 'I am thinking of a number. I add 6 and double the answer. The final answer is 16. What was the number I thought of?'

- This problem can be written as an equation using **brackets**.

  If the number thought of is x, then the first action is to add 6 giving $x + 6$. This answer is doubled which is written as $2(x + 6)$. The brackets are essential.
  The final equation is $2(x + 6) = 16$.

Example: Solve the equations **a** $2(x + 6) = 16$ **b** $3(x - 5) = 12$

a To solve this equation, you need x on its own on the left-hand side of the equals sign. You do this by **multiplying out** the brackets to give $2x + 12 = 16$.

First, eliminate '+ 12' by doing the inverse operation '− 12':

$2x = 4$

Now eliminate '× 2' by doing the inverse operation '÷ 2':

$x = 2$

b First expand the brackets, then add 15 and divide by 3:

$3x - 15 = 12$

$3x = 27$

$x = 9$

> **Top Tip!**
> There are different ways of writing the solution to an equation, but they all arrive at the same solution:
> $2(x + 6) = 16$
> $x + 6 = 8$ (divide by 2)
> $x = 2$ (subtract 6)

Equations with the letter on both sides of the equals sign

Example: Solve $3x + 6 = x + 10$

To solve this you need to have x on its own on the left-hand side of the equals sign. To do this, move all the x terms to the left-hand side and all the number terms to the right-hand side.

When a term moves over the equals sign its sign (plus or minus) changes:

$3x - x = 10 - 6$

Now tidy up the terms: $2x = 4$

and solve the equation: $x = 2$

Example: Solve $4x + 7 = 2x + 21$

Rearranging: $4x - 2x = 21 - 7$

Tidying up: $2x = 14$

Solving: $x = 7$

Check

Left-hand side = 4 × 7 + 7 = 35 ✓

Right-hand side = 2 × 7 + 21 = 35 ✓

> **Top Tip!**
> **Rearrange** the equation before working anything out. If you try to rearrange and work out at the same time, you are likely to make a mistake.

> **Top Tip!**
> Always check your answer in the original equation.

Sample National **Test question**

Solve the equations

a $4s + 7 = s + 25$

b $12x + 30 = 6x + 33$

Answers

a *Rearrange: $4s - s = 25 - 7$*

$3s = 18$

$s = 6$

Check $4 \times 6 + 7 = 31$, $6 + 25 = 31$, so LHS = RHS

b *Rearrange: $12x - 6x = 33 - 30$*

$6x = 3$

$x = \frac{1}{2}$

Check $12 \times \frac{1}{2} + 30 = 36$, $6 \times \frac{1}{2} + 33 = 36$, so LHS = RHS

Top Tip!

Always check that the left-hand side = right-hand side
LHS = RHS

Did You Know?

The equals symbol (=) was first used by Robert Recorde (*c*. 1510–1558) in 1557.

 **pot Check**

1 Solve the equations **a** $3(x - 8) = 15$ **b** $4x + 5 = 2x - 7$

2 Look at these cards.

 $2x - 1$ $\quad$ $5x + 1$ $\quad$ $3x + 7$ $\quad$ $3x + 1$

Card A $\quad$ Card B $\quad$ Card C $\quad$ Card D

a What value of x makes card A equal to 8?

b What value of x makes cards B and C equal?

c Explain why there is no value of x that works for both cards C and D.

Trial and improvement

Trial and improvement

- The only way to solve an equation like $x^3 + 2x = 27$ is by **trial and improvement**.
- Trial and improvement is just sensible **guesswork**.

Example: There is a solution of the equation
$x^3 + 2x = 27$ between 2 and 3.
Find the solution to 1 decimal place.

Start by making a guess between 2 and 3:

2.5 is a sensible guess.	$2.5^3 + 2 \times 2.5 = 20.625$
Then make a better guess:	$2.6^3 + 2 \times 2.6 = 22.776$
Keep on making better guesses:	$2.7^3 + 2 \times 2.7 = 25.083$
	$2.8^3 + 2 \times 2.8 = 27.552$

When you find two 1 decimal place values that 'bracket' the answer, check the middle value to make sure which of the values is closer.

$2.75^3 + 2 \times 2.75 = 26.296\ 875$

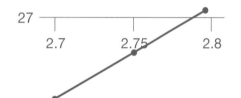

27

2.7   2.75   2.8

This means that 2.8 is the closer value to the answer.

Using a table to help you

- The best way to set out these problems is in a **table**. Tables are often given in National Test questions.

Example: Continue the table to solve the equation $x^3 - x = 50$

x	$x^3 - x$	Comment
4	60	Too high

First try the next number below 4, then keep on refining the guess.

x	$x^3 - x$	Comment
4	60	Too high
3	24	Too low
3.5	39.375	Too low
3.8	51.072	Too high
3.7	46.953	Too low
3.75	48.984375	Too low

The nearest 1 decimal place value is $x = 3.8$.

Sample National Test question

A rectangle has a side of length y centimetres.
The other side is of length $y + 3$ centimetres.

y cm

$y + 3$ cm

The area of the rectangle is 48.16 cm².
This equation shows the area of the rectangle:
$y(y + 3) = 48.16$
Find the value of y.

y	$y + 3$	$y(y + 3)$	Comment
4	7	28	Too low

Answer
The given starting value of 4 gives an area that is too low.

Continue the table with a higher value than 4.

y	$y + 3$	$y(y + 3)$	Comment
4	7	28	Too low
5	8	40	Too low
6	9	54	Too high
5.5	8.5	46.75	Too low
5.6	8.6	48.16	Exact

Because the answer is exact there is no need to test a halfway value.

Did You Know?
The longest trial in British history was the McLibel trial which lasted three years.

Spot Check

1 Show clearly why there is a solution of the equation $2x^3 + 3x = 100$ between $x = 3$ and $x = 4$.

SHAPE, SPACE AND MEASURES

Scales

Reading scales

- Scales occur in everyday life and come in a variety of different forms. They may be round, as on a weighing machine, or straight as on a thermometer. It is important to be able to read scales accurately.

Example: Read the values from the following scales. Do not forget the units.

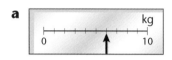

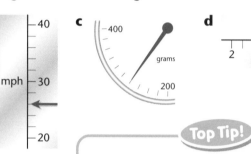

a 6 kg (the scale is marked in divisions of 1).

b 26 mph (the scale is marked in divisions of 2).

c 280 grams (the scale is marked in divisions of 20).

d 2.25 litres (the scale is marked in divisions of 0.1).

Top Tip!

Always check what each division represents. Also make sure which way the scale is reading. Normally scales read from left to right but some scales may read up, down, or right to left.

Timetables

- You should be able to read a clock face and a timetable.

Example: The timetable shows some times of the number 20 bus from Holmfirth to Penistone.

Holmfirth	Hade's Edge	Dunford Bridge	Victoria	Penistone
10:20	10:32	10:39	10:53	11:05
12:20	12:32	12:39	12:53	13:05
14:20	14:32	14:39	14:53	15:05

Top Tip!

Timetables always use the 24-hour clock. For example, 6 am is 06:00 and 1 pm is 13:00.

a How long is the journey from Holmfirth to Penistone?

b If I get to Dunford Bridge at 11:55 how long do I have to wait for a bus?

c John lives in Holmfirth and wants to catch a train in Penistone at 13:18.

   i Which bus should he catch?

   ii How long will he have in Penistone before the train leaves?

a All the buses take 45 minutes.

b 44 minutes. The next bus is at 12:39.

c *i* The 12:20 will get to Penistone at 13:05.

   ii 13 minutes from 13:05 to 13:18.

How many seconds are there in three minutes?

You should know that there are 60 seconds in one minute so there are 3 x 60 = 180 seconds in 3 minutes.

level
4

Sample National 💡 **Test question**

The clocks show the time that Kevin left his house and the time he returned.

a The digital clocks are showing the time in the 24-hour clock. How long was Kevin out of the house?

b Draw the time shown on the second digital clock on the ordinary clockface on the right.

Answers

a *From 09:20 to 13:25 is 4 hours and 5 minutes.*

b *The time is 1.25 pm so the clock will show:*

Did You Know?

Clocks in most jewellers' windows have their hands set to 10 to 2 so it looks like the clock is smiling.

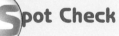

Spot Check

1 How long is there between 6.30 am and 14:05?

2 How much time has passed between the time on clock A and the time on clock B?

A    B

SHAPE, SPACE AND MEASURES

Metric units

Length

- The basic unit of **length** is the **metre** (m).
- Other common units for length are the **kilometre** (km), **centimetre** (cm) and **millimetre** (mm).

  10 mm = 1 cm

  100 cm = 1 m

  1000 m = 1 km

Example: How many metres is 1.3 kilometres?

1.3 km = 1.3 x 1000 = 1300 m

Example: How many centimetres is 54 millimetres?

54 mm = 54 ÷ 10 = 5.4 cm

> **Top Tip!**
> 2 metres is about the height of a normal doorway.

Mass

- **Mass** is the correct term for **weight**.
- The basic unit of mass is the **kilogram** (kg).
- Other common units for mass are the **gram** (g) and **tonne** (T).

  1000 g = 1 kg

  1000 kg = 1 T

Example: How many kilograms is $2\frac{1}{2}$ tonnes?

$2\frac{1}{2}$ T = $2\frac{1}{2}$ x 1000 = 2500 kg

> **Top Tip!**
> A normal bag of sugar weighs 1 kilogram. A 1p coin weighs $3\frac{1}{3}$ grams.

Capacity

- **Capacity** is also known as **volume**.
- The basic unit of capacity is the **litre** (l).
- Other common units for capacity are the **millilitre** (ml) and **centilitre** (cl).

  1000 ml = 1 l

  100 cl = 1 l

Example: How many litres is 450 centilitres?

450 cl = 450 ÷ 10 = 4.5 l

> **Top Tip!**
> A normal can of fizzy drink is about 330 ml or just over 3 cl.

How many metres is equivalent to 130 centimetres?

Divide by 100: 130 cm = 1.3 m

Learn what the prefixes mean:
milli- = ÷ 1000
centi- = ÷ 100
kilo- = x 1000

level
4

Sample National Test question

One large can and 4 small cans have a total mass of 4 kg.
The mass of the large can is 1.6 kg.
Each small can has the same mass.
What is the mass of one small can?
Give your answer in grams.

Answer
4 cans weigh 4 − 1.6 = 2.4 kg
1 can weighs 2.4 ÷ 4 = 0.6 kg
0.6 kg = 0.6 x 1000 = 600 g

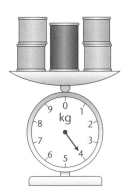

Top Tip!

If converting from a **larger** unit
to a **smaller** unit **multiply** by the
conversion factor. If converting from
a **smaller** unit to a **larger** unit
divide by the conversion factor.

Did You Know?

The metre was originally
defined as being one ten-
millionth part of a quarter of
the Earth's circumference.

**pot Check**

1 Which unit would you use to **sensibly** measure the following:
   a the width of a pencil
   b the capacity of a tea cup
   c the length of a car journey.

2 Convert
   a 3.4 metres to centimetres
   b 4500 millilitres to litres
   c 5 tonnes to kilograms
   d 98 millimetres to centimetres

SHAPE, SPACE AND MEASURES

Imperial units

levels 3-4

Imperial units

- Britain is slowly changing from imperial units to metric units, but some imperial units are still used to talk about height and weight.

I am 5ft 8in tall and weigh 11½ stone.

I am 1.52m tall and weigh 45kg.

levels 3-4

Units of length, weight and capacity

- Here are some imperial units that are still in common use:

Length	**Weight**	**Capacity**
12 in = 1 ft (foot)	16 oz = 1 lb (pronounced 'pound')	8 pints = 1 gallon
3 ft = 1 yd (yard)	14 lb = 1 st (stone)	

Top Tip!

You need to learn the approximations between imperial units and metric units. The symbol '≈' means 'is approximately equal to'.

levels 3-4

Conversion factors

- Here are some conversion factors that you need to know:

$1 \text{ m} \approx 3 \text{ ft}$	$1 \text{ in} \approx 2\frac{1}{2} \text{ cm}$	$1 \text{ kg} \approx 2\frac{1}{4} \text{ lb}$	$5 \text{ miles} \approx 8 \text{ km}$
$1 \text{ l} \approx 1\frac{3}{4} \text{ pints}$	$1 \text{ oz} \approx 30 \text{ g}$	$1 \text{ gallon} \approx 4\frac{1}{2} \text{ l}$	

Example: Estimate the distance to the hotel in metres.

Sunbeach Hotel 600 yards

$1 \text{ m} \approx 3 \text{ ft}$ and this also means $1 \text{ m} \approx 1 \text{ yd}$.
So 600 yards is approximately 600 metres.

Example: A man weighs $11\frac{1}{2}$ stone.

   a There are 14 lb in a stone.

     i How many pounds are there in $11\frac{1}{2}$ stone?

     ii Approximately how many kilograms is $11\frac{1}{2}$ stone?

   a i 11 stone = 11 x 14 = 154 lb and $\frac{1}{2}$ stone = 7 lb, so $11\frac{1}{2}$ stone = 161 lb.

     ii $161 \div 2\frac{1}{2} = 71.5$, so $11\frac{1}{2}$ stone ≈ 72 kg

Top Tip!

Always check that your answers are sensible by relating them to your real-life experience.

Top Tip!

If converting to a **bigger** unit, **divide** by the conversion factor (kg are bigger than pounds), and if converting to a **smaller** unit, **multiply** by the conversion factor (cm are smaller than inches).

Sample mental test question

Approximately how many kilometres is 15 miles?

5 miles ≈ 8 km, so 15 miles is about 24 km.

level
4

Sample National Test question

Dylan needs 8 gallons of petrol to fill the tank in his car.

Petrol
90p per litre

How much does he pay?

Answer
This has to be done in two steps.
Change 8 gallons into litres first:
1 gallon ≈ $4\frac{1}{2}$ litres, so 8 gallons ≈ 36 litres.
Now work out the cost:
36 x 90p = 3240p = £32.40

Did You Know?

Imperial units were originally based on parts of the body, so an inch was the length of the top joint of a thumb. A foot is obvious!

Spot Check

1 The baggage allowance on an airline is 20 kg. Will a case weighing 50 lb be within the allowance?

2 There are 12 inches in a foot.
  a How many inches is 5 ft 8 inches?
  b Approximately how many metres and centimetres are there in 5 ft 8 inches?

Measuring angles and bearings

levels 3-4

Measuring angles

• You need to know the names for the different types of angles:

An **acute angle** is between 0° and 90°.

A **right angle** is 90°.

An **obtuse angle** is between 90° and 180°.

A **straight line** is 180°.

A **reflex angle** is between 180° and 360°.

A **complete turn** is 360°.

Example: Measure the size of the acute angle.

Count the numbers round from 0° until you meet the second line of the angle. This acute angle is 55°.

Top Tip!

Remember to start from 0° and make sure the **centre** of the **protractor** is on the **point** of the angle.

level 6

Bearings

Example: Measure **i** the distance and **ii** the bearings of points A and B from the point O.

i First measure the distances OA and OB.

OA is 5 cm and OB is 3.5 cm.

This means that OA is 50 km and OB is 35 km.

ii Draw a North line and place a protractor with its centre at O and 0° along the North line.

Measure clockwise to find the bearings.
A is on a bearing of 100°.
B is on a bearing of 240°.

Scale 1 cm : 10 km

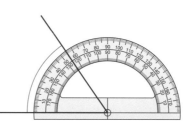

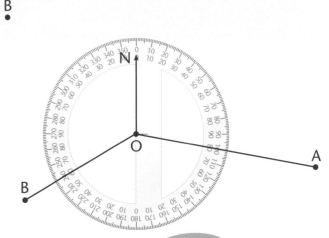

Top Tip!

A full round protractor is better for measuring bearings.

Top Tip!

Always start at **North** as zero degrees and measure **clockwise**. Bearings under 100° should be written with a zero in front e.g. 090°.

Sample mental test question

Look at the diagram.

Estimate the angle marked.

The angle is about 110°, so any answer from 100° to 120° would be an acceptable estimate.

Sample National Test question

Measure the size of each of the following angles.

a

b

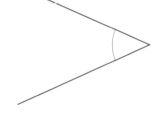

Answers
a *47°*
b *282°*

Did YOU Know?

The magnetic North Pole and the geographic North Pole are not the same place. They are about 3° apart if you are in Britain.

 **Spot Check**

1 What is **a** an obtuse angle **b** a reflex angle?

2 What bearing is **a** East **b** South **c** West?

SHAPE, SPACE AND MEASURES

Angle facts

Angles on lines and around points

- You need to know how to use these angle facts:

  Angles on a **straight line** add up to 180°.

  Angles at a **point** add up to 360°.

Example: Find the angles marked x and y.

$x + 53 = 180$

$x = 180 - 53 = 127°$

$y + 115 + 90 = 360$

$y = 360 - 115 - 90 = 155°$

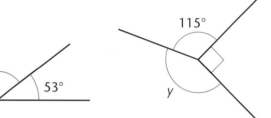

Angles in polygons

- You need to know some angle facts about **polygons**.

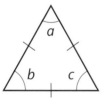 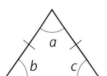 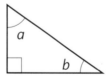

The three **interior** angles in a **triangle** add up to 180°. $a + b + c = 180°$

The four **interior** angles in a **quadrilateral** add up to 360°. $a + b + c + d = 360°$

The **exterior** angle of a triangle equals the **sum** of the **two opposite interior** angles. $a + b = c$

Special triangles

Equilateral triangle
$a = b = c = 60°$

Isosceles triangle
$b = c$

Right-angled triangle $a + b = 90°$

Top Tip!

The small dashes marked on lines show that those lines are of the same length

Example: Find the angles marked with letters in these shapes.

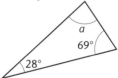 

$a + 28 + 69 = 180$

$a + 97 = 180$

$a = 180 - 97$

$a = 83°$

$b + 98 + 102 + 90 = 360$

$b + 290 = 360$

$b = 360 - 290$

$b = 70°$

angle on base = $180 - 110$

$= 70$

$c + 70 + 70 = 180$

$c = 40°$

Sample mental test question

Two angles in a triangle are 45° and 85°. How many degrees is the other angle?

Work out 45 + 85 and then take the answer away from 180.

45 + 85 = 130

180 – 130 = 50

The angle is 50˚.

Sample National Test question

Find the size of the missing angles on each diagram.

a
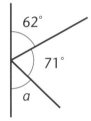

62°
71°
a

b
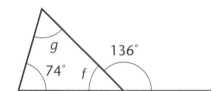

g
136°
74° f

Top Tip!

Diagrams like these in the National Tests are never drawn accurately so do not measure them with a protractor.

Answers

a   *a + 62 + 71 = 180*

  a + 133 = 180

  a = 47°

b   *f + 136 = 180*

  f = 44°

  g + 74 = 136

  g = 62°

Did YOU Know?

When mud dries in the sun, the cracks form curves that intersect at right angles.

Spot Check

1 What is the missing angle in this triangle?

x
18°

2 Find the missing angles on this diagram.

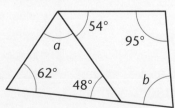

54°
95°
a
62°
48° b

59

SHAPE, SPACE AND MEASURES
Angles in parallel lines and polygons

Intersecting lines and angles in parallel lines

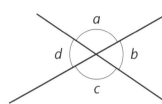

In these intersecting lines, vertically opposite angles are equal.

$a = c$ and $b = d$

- Parallel lines never meet. They provide some special types of angles.

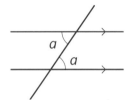

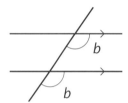

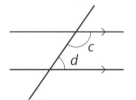

Alternate angles are **equal**.

Corresponding angles are **equal**.

Interior angles add up to **180°**.

$c + d = 180°$

Example: Find the angles marked by letters.

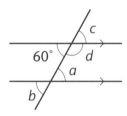

$a = 60°$ (alternate angle)

$b = 60°$ (vertically opposite angle to a)

$c = 60°$ (corresponding angle to a)

$d = 120°$ (interior angle to a)

Top Tip!

Alternate angles: look for a 'Z'.
Corresponding angles: look for an 'F'.
Interior angles: look for a 'C'.

Polygons

- Polygons are two-dimensional (**2-D**) shapes with **straight** sides.

Name of polygon	Number of sides	Sum of interior angles
Triangle	3	180°
Quadrilateral	4	360°
Pentagon	5	540°
Hexagon	6	720°
Heptagon	7	900°
Octagon	8	1080°

Top Tip!

When solving angle problems, always give a reason for how you found each angle.
Always use the correct mathematical words:
- alternate angles
- corresponding angles
- interior angles.

- A pentagon can be split into three triangles, so the sum of the five interior angles is 3 x 180° = 540°.

Regular polygons

- **Regular polygons** are polygons with **all sides equal** and **all angles equal**.

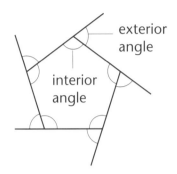

exterior
angle

interior
angle

The regular pentagon has five equal interior angles
and five equal exterior angles.

Sum of the five exterior angles = 360°

So each exterior angle = 72°

Interior angle + exterior angle = 180°

Each interior angle = 108°

Sample National Test question

ABCD is a rectangle.
Find the angles marked with a letter.

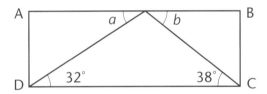

Answers
AB is parallel to CD, so a =32° (alternate angle)
and b = 38° (alternate angle).

Did You Know?

Islamic art is based
on polygons, which
can be constructed
with circles.

Spot Check

1 Find the angles *a* and *b* in this regular hexagon.

2 Find the missing angles in this diagram.

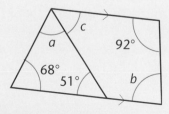

SHAPE, SPACE AND MEASURES

Symmetry

levels 3-4

Line symmetry

- With line symmetry, you can draw a line across a shape and both halves will fold exactly together.
- The line is called a **mirror line** or a **line of symmetry**.

Top Tip!

You can use a mirror or tracing paper to check for a line of symmetry.

Example: How many lines of symmetry have the following shapes?

 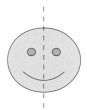 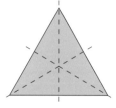

No lines of symmetry   1 line of symmetry   2 lines of symmetry   3 lines of symmetry

levels 3-4

Rotational symmetry

- With rotational symmetry, you can turn the shape into different positions that all look exactly the same.
- The number of different positions is called the **order of rotational symmetry**.

Example: What is the order of rotational symmetry for the following shapes?

Order 1   Order 2   Order 4   Order 8

Top Tip!

Rotational symmetry of order 1 is the same as saying 'no rotational symmetry'. You can give either answer.

Top Tip!

You can use tracing paper to check for rotational symmetry.
You can use tracing paper in the Tests.

Spot Check

1 a How many lines of symmetry has this shape got?

b What is the order of rotational symmetry?

2 Write down the number of lines of symmetry of each of these shapes:

a   **b**   **c**

Quadrilaterals

Example: Write down the symmetry properties of these quadrilaterals.

Square

4 lines of symmetry
Rotational symmetry
of order 4

Rectangle

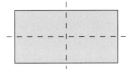

2 lines of symmetry
Rotational symmetry
of order 2

Parallelogram

0 lines of symmetry
Rotational symmetry
of order 2

Rhombus

2 lines of symmetry
Rotational symmetry
of order 2

Kite

1 line of symmetry
Rotational symmetry
of order 1

Trapezium

0 lines of symmetry
Rotational symmetry
of order 1

Sample mental test question

Look at the shape.
Complete the picture
so that the dotted line
is a line of symmetry.

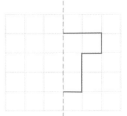

*Draw the other half
of the shape.*

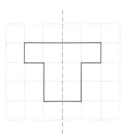

Sample National Test question

Shade three more squares so that the grid
has rotational symmetry of order 2.

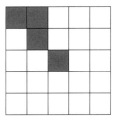

Answer

Did You Know?

Palindromes are words or
phrases that read the
same backwards as
forwards, such as 'I prefer
pi' or 'Madam, I'm Adam'.

SHAPE, SPACE AND MEASURES

Reflections and rotations

Reflections

- A **reflection** creates a **mirror image** of a given object.

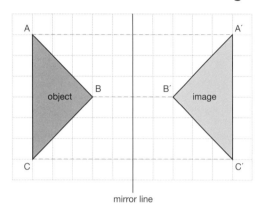

mirror line

If you trace the object and the image and fold along the mirror line,

the two shapes should be exactly over each other.

- The object triangle ABC has been reflected in the mirror line to give the image triangle A'B'C'.

- The blue dashed lines show that any point on the object and its corresponding image point are the same distance from the mirror line. The line joining the two points also crosses the mirror line at right angles.

Rotations

- A **rotation** turns the object through a given angle about a point called the **centre of rotation**.

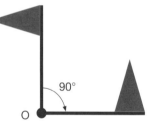

90°

O

Top Tip!

You can always use tracing paper to check your rotation.

- The flag has been rotated through 90° clockwise about the centre of rotation O.

Spot Check

1 Draw the reflection of the triangle in the dotted line.

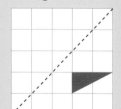

Top Tip!

Turn the page round so the mirror line is horizontal or vertical.

This makes it easier to see the reflection.

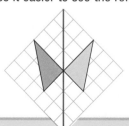

Congruency

- In both reflections and rotations, the object and the image are **identical** in their **size** and **shape**. We say that the two shapes are **congruent**.

Example: Which two of the shapes below are congruent?

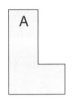 A B C D

Top Tip!

Congruent means 'exactly the same shape and size'.
Similar means 'the same shape but different sizes'.

B and D. A is the same shape as B but bigger. C is not the same shape. D is the same shape as B but rotated and reflected.

Sample mental test question

Look at the grid. Shape A has been rotated clockwise about the point O to make shape B.

What is the angle of rotation?

Using tracing paper, or just by looking, you can see that the angle of rotation is 90°.

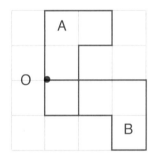

Sample National Test questions

a Reflect the triangle in the mirror line.

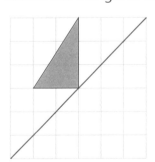

b Rectangle A has been rotated onto rectangle B about the point O. Describe the rotation.

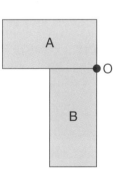

Answers

a

b *Rectangle A can move clockwise or anticlockwise, so there are two answers: a rotation of 90° anticlockwise or a rotation of 270° clockwise.*

Did You Know?

The Earth rotates once every day. Venus rotates once every 243 Earth days. Nights on Venus can be very long!

SHAPE, SPACE AND MEASURES

Enlargements

Scale factor

- An **enlargement** changes the **size** of a shape.
- The **scale factor** tells you **how many times bigger** the shape is to be enlarged.
- The shape will stay the same but the sides will all increase by the same factor.

Example: Shapes B and C are enlargements of shape A.
What is the scale factor of each enlargement?

Compare the lengths of any two
common sides.
Shape B has a scale factor of $1\frac{1}{2}$.
Shape C has a scale factor of 2.

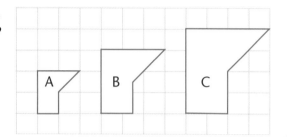

Centre of enlargement

- To enlarge a shape, you also need a **centre of enlargement**.

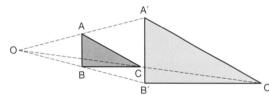

Triangle ABC is enlarged by a scale factor of 2 about the centre of enlargement O.
All the sides are doubled in length.

OA' = 2 x OA

OB' = 2 x OB

OC' = 2 x OC

Notice that all the measurements are from O.

Example: Enlarge the triangle ABC about
the origin O by a scale factor of 3.

The coordinates of the vertices of triangle
ABC are: A(3, 2), B(3, 1) and C(1, 1).

The coordinates of the vertices of triangle
A'B'C' are: A'(9, 6), B'(9, 3) and C'(3, 3).

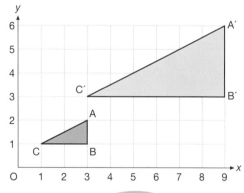

Top Tip!

If you draw lines through
common vertices, they
will meet at the centre of
enlargement.

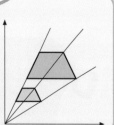

Top Tip!

The coordinates of the vertices of triangle
ABC above are multiplied by the scale factor
to give the vertices of triangle A'B'C'. This
method works if the centre of enlargement is
at the origin, but not if it is elsewhere.

Sample National Test question

Enlarge the trapezium ABCD by a scale factor of 2 about the origin O.

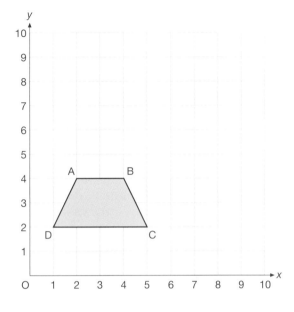

Answer

The coordinates of the enlarged trapezium A'B'C'D' are:

A'(4, 8), B'(8, 8), C'(10, 4) and D'(2, 4).

Did You Know?

If you place a sheet of paper on the floor and keep doubling the size of the pile, i.e. 1 sheet becomes 2, 2 sheets become 4 etc., after 50 doubles the pile will be 100 million kilometres high.

**pot Check**

1 Enlarge this triangle by a scale factor of 3.

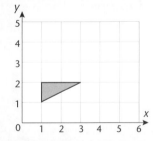

2 Triangle A has been enlarged to give triangle B. Find the scale factor and centre of enlargement.

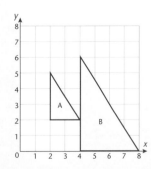

SHAPE, SPACE AND MEASURES

3-D shapes

level 5

Polyhedra

- **2-D** shapes are called **polygons** and **3-D** shapes are called **polyhedra**.
- These are the names of the 3-D shapes you need to know.

Cube

Cuboid

Square-based pyramid

Tetrahedron

Triangular prism

Cylinder

Cone

Sphere

- A **cuboid** has 12 **edges**, 8 **vertices** and 6 **faces**.

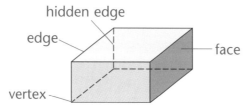

Nets

level 5

- A **net** is a 2-D shape that can be folded to make a 3-D shape.

Example: This is a net for a square-based pyramid.

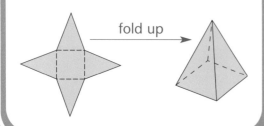
fold up

Plans and elevations

level 5

- A **plan** is a view of a 3-D shape **from above**.
- An **elevation** is a view of a 3-D shape from **one side**.

Example: These are the views for a triangular prism.

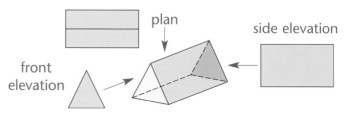

Spot Check

1 Which of the following are nets for a cube?

A

B

C

D

Isometric drawings

- 3-D shapes drawn on isometric paper are more accurate and measurements can be taken from the diagram.

Example: This is the isometric drawing for a cuboid:

Top Tip!

When using isometric paper, the dots should form columns:

i.e.

not

Planes of symmetry

- A 3-D shape has **plane symmetry** if it can be **cut in half** so that one half is a **mirror image** of the other half.

Example: A cuboid has three planes of symmetry.

Sample National Test question

The diagram shows a shape made from 5 one centimetre cubes.
On the grid below draw:
a the plan   **b** the elevation from X.

Answers

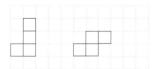

Did You Know?

Elevation is another term for height above sea level. Lake Titicaca is the highest lake in the world with an elevation of 3810 m. The Dead Sea is the lowest with an elevation of −411 m.

SHAPE, SPACE AND MEASURES

Perimeter and area

level 4

Perimeter

- **Perimeter** is the total **distance around** the outside of a 2-D shape.

Example: Find the perimeter of this shape.

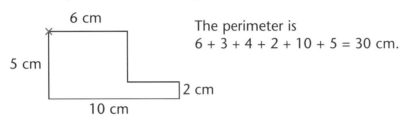

The perimeter is
6 + 3 + 4 + 2 + 10 + 5 = 30 cm.

Top Tip!
When finding a perimeter, put a mark on one vertex (corner) and count round the sides until you get back to the start.

level 3

Area

- **Area** is the **amount of space** inside a 2-D shape.
- The common units for area are: mm², cm² or m².

level 3

Area by counting squares

Example: Estimate the area of this shape.

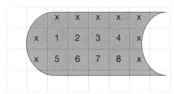

First count the number of whole squares. Then mark the squares where the area is more than half a square. An estimate for the area is $8 + 9 \times \frac{1}{2} = 12\frac{1}{2}$ cm².

level 4

Area of a rectangle

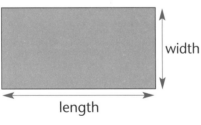

Example: Find the area of this rectangle.

- Area = length x width
  $A = l \times w$
  $A = lw$

$A = lw = 12 \times 5 = 60$ m²

Top Tip!
Make sure you always write the correct units for area.

Spot Check

1 What is the perimeter and area of this shape?

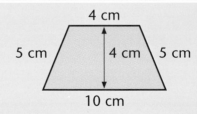

Area formulae

- In these formulae, b stands for 'base' and h stands for 'height' although the correct term is 'perpendicular height'.

Parallelogram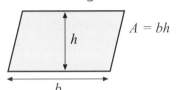

$A = bh$

Triangle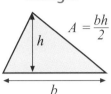

$A = \dfrac{bh}{2}$

Trapezium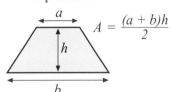

$A = \dfrac{(a + b)h}{2}$

Example: Find the area of these shapes.

a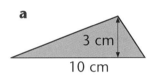

3 cm

10 cm

b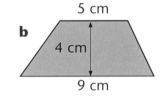

5 cm

4 cm

9 cm

a $A = \dfrac{bh}{2} = \dfrac{10 \times 3}{2} = 15$ cm²   **b** $A = \dfrac{(a + b)h}{2} = \dfrac{(9 + 5) \times 4}{2} = 28$ cm²

Top Tip!

Do not try to work these out in your head. Always substitute numbers into the formula. You will have more chance of reaching the correct answer.

Sample mental 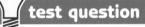 test question

A square has an area of 36 cm².
What is the perimeter of the square?

The length of a side of the square is 6 cm, since 6 x 6 = 36.
The perimeter of the square is 4 x 6 = 24 cm.

Sample National  Test question

On a grid, draw a triangle that has an area of 6 cm².

Answer
Possible triangles are:

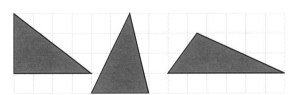

Did You Know?

On average there are about 4000 square metres of land for every person in Britain. That's less than a soccer pitch.

SHAPE, SPACE AND MEASURES
Circumference and area of a circle

level 6

Circumference of a circle

- The **circumference** is the **perimeter** of a circle.
- You need to know that $d = 2 \times r$.

radius, r

centre

O

diameter, d

There are two formulae for the circumference of a circle:

- Circumference = 2 x π x radius

  $C = 2\pi r$

- Circumference = π x diameter

  $C = \pi d$

- π = 3.14 to 2 decimal places or use the π key on your calculator.

Example: Calculate the circumference of this circle.

8 cm

$C = \pi d = \pi \times 8 = 25.1$ cm (1 d.p.)

 Key sequence on your calculator:

π × 8 =

Top Tip!

Always give your answer to 1 decimal place (1 d.p.) unless the question says otherwise.

level 6

Area of a circle

- Area = π x radius²

  $A = \pi \times r \times r$

  $A = \pi r^2$

Top Tip!

Questions will give either the radius or diameter. Make sure you use the correct value in the appropriate formula.

Example: Calculate the area of this circle.

7 cm

Top Tip!

Write down the formula first and always show your working.

$A = \pi r^2 = \pi \times 7^2 = 153.9$ cm² (1 d.p.)

 Key sequence on your calculator:

π × 7 x^2 =

Top Tip!

Always square the radius before you multiply by π.

Sample National  Test questions

a James' bike wheel has a radius of
30 cm. Calculate its circumference,
giving your answer to the nearest
centimetre.

b The circle and the square have the same area.

4 cm

x

Calculate x, the length of the side of the square.

a $r = 30$ cm , so $d = 60$ cm.
$C = \pi d = \pi \times 60 = 188$ cm (nearest cm)

b The area of the circle is $A = \pi r^2 = \pi \times 4^2 = 50.26...$
So $x = \sqrt{50.26...} = 7.1$ cm (1 d.p.)

Did You Know?

In early 2006 Chris Lyons
from Australia recited the
first 4400 digits of pi
from memory.

pot Check

1 What is the circumference and
area of this circle?

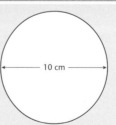

10 cm

2 A circular pond has a diameter
of 6 metres.
A one metre path is built around
the outside of the pond.
What is the area of the path?

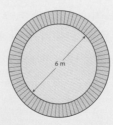

6 m

SHAPE, SPACE AND MEASURES

Volume

Volume

- **Volume** is the **amount of space** inside a **3-D** shape.
- The common units for volume are: mm^3, cm^3 or m^3.

Volume of a cuboid

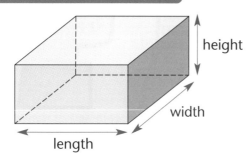

height

width

length

- Volume = length x width x height

$V = l \text{ x } w \text{ x } h$

$V = lwh$

Example: Find the volume of this cuboid.

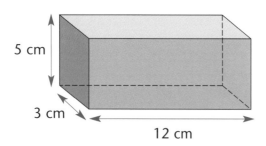

5 cm

3 cm

12 cm

$V = lwh$

$= 12 \text{ x } 3 \text{ x } 5 = 180 \text{ cm}^3.$

Top Tip!

Substitute numbers into a formula before trying to work anything out.

Surface area of a cuboid

- There are 6 **faces** on a cuboid, with opposite faces having the same area.
- The **surface area** is given by

$A = 2lw + 2lh + 2wh$

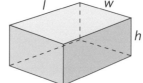

l   *w*

h

Example: Find the surface area of the purple cuboid in the panel above.

$A = 2 \text{ x } 12 \text{ x } 3 + 2 \text{ x } 12 \text{ x } 5 + 2 \text{ x } 3 \text{ x } 5 = 72 + 120 + 30 = 222 \text{ cm}^2.$

Capacity

- **Capacity** is the **amount of space** inside a **hollow 3-D** shape.
- Capacity usually refers to the volume of a gas or liquid. You need to know 1000 cm³ = 1 litre.

Example: Find the volume of this fish tank, giving your answer in litres.

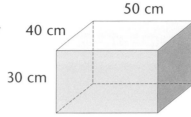

V = 50 x 40 x 30
= 60 000 cm³
V = 60 litres

Example: This is a net of a cuboid. If one square has an area of 1 cm², what is the volume of the cuboid?

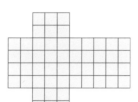

V = 4 x 3 x 2 = 24 cm³

Sample mental test question

The volume of a cube is 27 cm³.
What is the length of an edge of the cube?

Since 27 = 3 x 3 x 3, the length of an edge = 3 cm.

Top Tip!

You should know these cube roots:
$\sqrt[3]{1} = 1$
$\sqrt[3]{8} = 2$
$\sqrt[3]{27} = 3$
$\sqrt[3]{64} = 4$
$\sqrt[3]{125} = 5$
$\sqrt[3]{1000} = 10$

Sample National Test question

These two cuboids have the same volume.
Find the value of *x*.

3 cm, 3 cm, 3 cm, 4 cm

3 cm, 2 cm, *x*

Answer
Volume of first cuboid = 36 cm³.
Volume of second cuboid = 6x = 36 cm³.
So x = 6 cm.

Did You Know?
The volume of the Sun can hold over a million Earths.

**pot Check**

1 What is the volume and surface area of this cuboid?

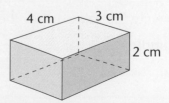

4 cm, 3 cm, 2 cm

HANDLING DATA · Statistics

Statistics

- Statistics involves collecting and interpreting **data**.
- Data is best collected by carrying out **surveys** or by using **questionnaires**.
- Data can be sorted easily by putting it into a table called a **tally chart** or a **frequency table**.

Example: This frequency table shows the scores when a dice has been thrown 30 times.

Score	Tally	Frequency
1	ⅢⅡ	6
2	Ⅲ	5
3					3
4	Ⅲ ||	7
5	Ⅲ	5
6						4
	Total	30

Top Tip!

Note the tallies. Single marks are used for totals of 1 to 4 and a 'gate' is used for a total of 5.

Mode and range

- The **mode** for a set of data is the value that occurs **most often**.

  From the frequency table above, the score that occurs most often is 4. So we say the mode of the scores is 4 or the modal score is 4.

- The **range** for a set of data is calculated as: **the highest value – the lowest value.**

  From the frequency table, the range of the scores is 6 – 1 = 5.

Example: Find the mode and range of this data: 3, 5, 7, 4, 3, 2, 5, 8, 9, 10, 2, 3, 6, 4

  The value that occurs the most often (mode) is 3.
  The range is the difference between highest and lowest: 10 – 2 = 8.

Bar charts

- Data can be represented on various diagrams, such as a **bar chart**.
- When drawing a bar chart always remember to:
  - label the axes
  - leave gaps between the bars
  - write the values below the middle of each bar.

Example: This bar chart shows the scores on the dice for the frequency table above.

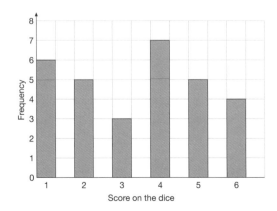

Sample mental 💡 test question

Look at the data shown: 5, 2, 10, 5, 5.

What is the range of the data?

The range is 10 – 2 = 8.

Sample National 💡 Test question

Here are the numbers of goals scored by a team in 20 games.

0　1　0　1　1　2　1　3　2　4

0　1　3　4　2　0　1　1　0　2

a　Draw a frequency table to show the scores.

b　What is the mode for the number of goals scored?

c　What is the range of the number of goals scored?

Answers

a

Score	Tally	Frequency
0	✝✝✝	5
1	✝✝✝ ‖	7
2	‖‖‖	4
3	‖	2
4	‖	2
	Total	20

b　*The mode is 1 goal.*

c　*The range is 4 – 0 = 4 goals.*

Did You Know?

The average bed is home to over 6 billion dust mites.

 **Spot Check**

1 Find the mode and range of the data shown in the bar chart. It shows the number of people in 10 cars.

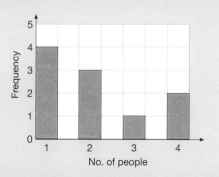

HANDLING DATA

Mode, median and mean

levels
3-4

The mode

- An **average** is a typical value for a set of data.
- The **mode** of a set of data is the value that occurs **most often**.

Example: Find the mode for this set of data.
10   13   14   10   13   10   15   16
The mode is 10.

> **Top Tip!**
>
> **MOde** = **MO**st common
> **Median** = **Med**ium (middle)
> **Mean** = the 'nastiest' because it is the hardest to work out!

levels
3-4

The median

- To find the **median** for a set of data, first put the values in order from smallest to largest, and then pick out the exact **middle** value.

Example: Find the median for this set of data.
6   5   9   2   6   4   7   8   3
In order: 2   3   4   5   6   6   7   8   9
The median is 6.

Example: The ages of six people are: 21, 32, 25, 19, 23 and 18.
Find their median age.
In order: 18   19   21   23   25   32
There are two numbers in the middle, so the median is the number halfway between 21 and 23. The median is 22.

> **Top Tip!**
>
> If data is not in order, it must be put in order.

levels
5-6

The mean

- To find the **mean** for a set of data, first find the **total** of all the **values** and then **divide** this total by the **number of values**.

The symbol for the mean is $\bar{x}$. $\bar{x} = \dfrac{\text{Total of all values}}{\text{Number of values}}$

Example: The ages of six people are: 21, 32, 25, 19, 23 and 18. Find their mean age.

 $\bar{x} = \dfrac{\text{Total of all values}}{\text{Number of values}} = \dfrac{138}{6} = 23$

 **Spot Check**   **1** Find the mode, median and mean for this set of data.
19, 24, 24, 18, 22, 24, 27, 18

The mean and median from a frequency table

- To find the mean from a frequency table, add an extra column to find the total of all the values.

Example: The frequency table shows the marks for 20 students in a spelling test. Find the mean mark and the median mark.

Mark, x	Frequency, f	$x \times f$
5	1	5
6	0	0
7	3	21
8	5	40
9	8	72
10	3	30
Totals	**20**	**168**

$$\overline{x} = \frac{\text{Total of all values}}{\text{Number of values}} = \frac{168}{20} = 8.4 \text{ (mean)}$$

The median is between the 10th and 11th values. Counting up the frequency column gives 10th and 11th values as 9. Median = 9.

Top Tip!

If the mean is not an exact answer, then round it to 1 decimal place.

Sample mental test question

What is the mean of 19, 21, 23 and 37?

Add the numbers together: 19 + 21 + 23 + 37 = 100 $\overline{x} = 100 \div 4 = 25$

Sample National Test question

a Find the mean of the numbers on these cards.

b Another card is added and the mean goes up by 2.
What number is on the new card?

Answers

a The mean = (3 + 4 + 6 + 7) ÷ 4 = 20 ÷ 4 = 5
b The new mean is 7, so the five numbers add up to 35.
The number on the new card is 35 − 20 = 15.

Did You Know?

The average person in the UK spends 18 hours a week watching TV.

Comparing distributions

- You compare distributions in everyday situations, without even realising it.

Example: Two dinner ladies, Mary and Doris, serve chips in the school canteen.

mmm... ChipS!

Rajid went to Mary for his chips for a week. Mary gave out 18, 23, 25, 25, 34 chips.

The following week Rajid went to Doris for his chips. Doris gave out 23, 25, 27, 25, 25 chips.

Which dinner lady should Rajid go to to be given the most chips?

First, look at the averages and range:

	Mean	Median	Mode	Range
Mary	25	25	25	16
Doris	25	25	25	4

The averages are all the same but Mary's range is much larger than Doris'. So if Rajid caught Mary on a good day, he might have as many as 34 chips, but on a bad day he might have as few as 18. Doris is very consistent and will always give about 25 chips.

You could say, 'The averages are the same' and 'I would go to Mary as she has a bigger range and you might be lucky and get a lot of chips', or you could say, 'I would go to Doris because she has a smaller range and is more consistent'. It doesn't matter who you choose as long as you mention the **average** and the **range** and give **reasons** for your choice.

Top Tip! The **range** measures the spread of the data so gives an indication of how **consistent** the data is.

Top Tip! When comparing data using ranges and averages, you must **refer** to them both in your answer.

Example: John records the lateness of two school buses A and B.

Over a week, bus A is 0, 2, 5, 7 and 1 minute late.
Over the same week, bus B is 2, 4, 2, 4, 3 minutes late.

a Work out the mean and range for bus A.
b Work out the mean and range for bus B.
c Which bus is more reliable?
   Give reasons for your answer.

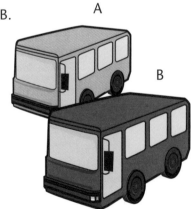

A
B

a Mean = (0 + 2 + 5 + 7 + 1) ÷ 5 = 15 ÷ 5 = 3 minutes
   Range = 7 − 0 = 7 minutes
b Mean = (2 + 4 + 2 + 4 + 3) ÷ 5 = 15 ÷ 5 = 3 minutes
   Range = 4 − 2 = 2 minutes
c Both buses have the same mean but bus B has a smaller range so is more consistent. Bus B is more reliable even though it is always late.

Top Tip! Compare the averages, even if they are the same. Also compare the ranges.

Give three numbers with a mode of 5 and a range of 2.

If there are three numbers and 5 is the mode, then two of the numbers must be 5. To give a range of 2, the other number must be 3 or 7. So there are two answers: 3, 5, 5 or 5, 5, 7.

level
6

Sample National  Test question

Jayne needs to pick an attacker for the netball team.
She looks at the scoring record of Asha and Rhoda.
In Asha's last five matches she scored 5, 7, 2, 9, 2 goals.
In Rhoda's last five matches she scored 5, 6, 5, 4, 5 goals.
Who should Jayne choose and why?

Answer
The averages for Asha are: Mode 2, Median 5, Mean 5.
The averages for Rhoda are: Mode 5, Median 5, Mean 5.
The range of Asha's scores is 9 − 2 = 7.
The range of Rhoda's scores is 6 − 4 = 2.
The averages are the same, except for the modes, but Rhoda has a smaller range so she is more consistent.
Although Asha may get a high score, she may also get a low score so Jayne should pick Rhoda.

Did You Know?

On an average work day, a typist's fingers travel 20 kilometres over a range of 20 cm.

 **Spot Check**

1 Work out the mean and range of these two sets of data.

a 4, 6, 6, 9, 10

b 2, 5, 7, 8, 13

HANDLING DATA — Line graphs

level 5

Plotting values

- A **line graph** is a clear way of showing **changes in data**.

Example: The maximum temperature in a town each month for a year is recorded.

Jan	Feb	Mar	Apr	May	Jun	Jul	Aug	Sep	Oct	Nov	Dec
4	9	13	19	25	28	32	29	22	17	13	7

a Which two months had a maximum temperature of 13 °C?

b Which was the hottest month?

c What is the difference between the hottest and coldest months?

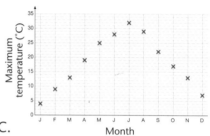

a Reading across from 13 °C on the y-axis gives the two months as March and November.

b July was the hottest month with a maximum temperature of 32 °C.

c January was the coldest month with a maximum temperature of 4 °C so the difference is 32 − 4 = 28 °C.

level 5

Trend lines

- You can see from the graph above that the temperature rises in summer. If we join the points, the lines between them have no meaning but they show the trend of the temperatures over the year.

Example: The graph below shows Sam's height from the age of 2 to the age of 8.

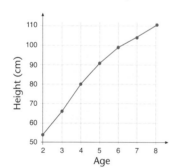

a How many centimetres did Sam grow from the age of 2 to 8?

b Is it possible to estimate Sam's age at $3\frac{1}{2}$ years old?

a Sam was 54 cm at age 2 and 110 cm at age 8 so he grew 56 cm.

b Yes, growth is continuous so the line has a meaning this time. Sam was about 74 cm tall at age $3\frac{1}{2}$.

Example: The following graph shows the monthly gas use for the Henman family.

a During which month was the most gas used?

b During one of the months in the summer the Henman family went on holiday. Which month was this? Give a reason for your answer.

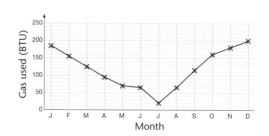

a The most gas was used during December as this is the highest value on the graph.

b July. The amount of gas drops dramatically in July suggesting that the family were not at home.

Sample National Test question

Jason records the temperature in his greenhouse once an hour. At 8 am it was 14 °C, at 9 am it was 20 °C, at 10 am it was 25 °C and at 11 am it was 29 °C.

This information is shown on the graph.

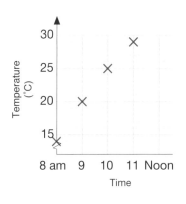

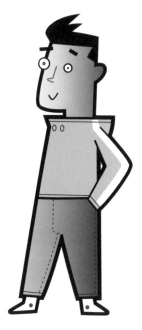

Top Tip!

You can **estimate** values from trend lines but you cannot say for sure what the values are.

a   Estimate the temperature at 10.30 am.

b   Explain why the graph cannot be used to predict the temperature at 12 noon.

Answers

a   *Using the trend line between 10 am and 11 am, the temperature can be estimated as 27 °C.*

b   *The trend line may not continue after 11 am. The sun could go in, or the windows could be opened.*

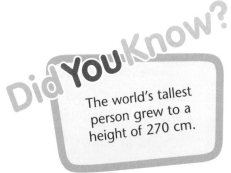

Did **YOU Know?**

The world's tallest person grew to a height of 270 cm.

Spot Check

1   The temperature drops by 4 °C from 5 am to 6 am. It was 7 °C at 5 am.

    a   What was the approximate temperature at 5.30 am?

    b   Can you estimate the temperature at 7 am?

2   Using the graph of Sam's height on the opposite page, decide during which years Sam grew the fastest. Explain how you can tell.

Reading pie charts

• You need to be able to read and draw pie charts. The main thing to remember is that frequencies are represented by **angles** and that the **total frequency** will be equivalent to **360°**.

Example: This pie chart shows the favourite colours of Class 9A. If 5 students choose blue as their favourite colour, how many students are in Class 9A?

Favourite colours of Class 9A

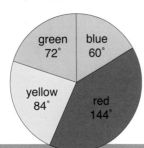

There are 5 students represented by 60°.
1 student is represented by 60 ÷ 5 = 12°.
There are 360° in the circle, and 360 ÷ 12 = 30.
There are 30 students, in the class.

Top Tip!

Always **label** pie charts and give a **title** to show what the pie chart represents.

Pie charts and frequencies

Example: This table shows the types of vehicles parked in a motorway service area.

Type of vehicle	Frequency
Car	40
Vans	22
Motorbikes	8
Lorries	20

Draw a pie chart to show the data.

First add up the frequencies: they total 90.

Divide this into 360 to find the angle that represents each vehicle: 360 ÷ 90 = 4°.

Now multiply each frequency by this figure. This is easily shown by adding another column to the table.

Type of vehicle	Frequency	Angle
Car	40	40 x 4 = 160°
Vans	22	22 x 4 = 88°
Motorbikes	8	8 x 4 = 32°
Lorries	20	20 x 4 = 80°

Then start with a circle, draw a radius and measure each angle in turn.

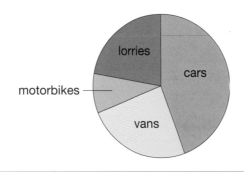

Top Tip!

It is useful to know the factors of 360:

1 x 360	8 x 45
2 x 180	9 x 40
3 x 120	10 x 36
4 x 90	12 x 30
5 x 72	15 x 24
6 x 60	18 x 20

Sample mental  test question

The pie chart shows the ratio of men to women at a concert.

If 2000 people attended, how many women were there?

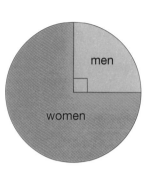

You can see from the pie chart that 75% of the people were women, 75% of 2000 = 1500.

Sample National  Test question

The pie chart shows the results of a survey about where families went for their holidays.

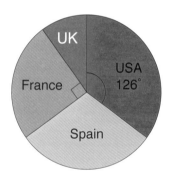

The sector for the USA represents 7 families.
How many families went to France?

Answer

There are 126° representing the USA sector.

7 families = 126°, so 1 family = 126 ÷ 7 = 18°.

There are 360 ÷ 18 = 20 families in the survey.

France is a quarter of the pie chart,
so 20 ÷ 4 = 5 families went to France.

Did You Know?

Every few years the village of Denby Dale in Yorkshire bakes a big meat pie. The last was the Millennium Pie in 2000 which was claimed to weigh 12 tonnes. However, nobody will admit to have seen it and the *Guinness Book of Records* doesn't recognise it.

Spot Check

1 If 7 out of 30 people prefer coffee, what angle would coffee have on a pie chart showing people's favourite drinks?

2 The 'dog' sector of a pie chart representing the favourite pets of a class has an angle of 20°.

   a Explain why there could not be 30 students in the class.

   b How many students could there have been in the class?

Grouped data

- When there is a lot of data covering a wide range, you may collect it using groups.

Example: This table shows the marks for Year 11 in their mathematics mock exam.

Mark, m	Frequency, f
$20 < m \leq 30$	7
$30 < m \leq 40$	29
$40 < m \leq 50$	56
$50 < m \leq 60$	32
$60 < m \leq 70$	15
$70 < m \leq 80$	8
$80 < m \leq 90$	3

$20 < m \leq 30$ means marks that are greater than 20 and less than, or equal to, 30.

- If you add up all the frequencies, you can tell that 150 students took the examination.

- However, you cannot tell exactly what any of the following are: the lowest mark, the highest mark, the mode, the median, the range or the exact mean.

Types of data

- **Continuous data** is data that can take **any value** with a **range**. For example, height of plants, weight of cattle and speed of cars.

- **Discrete data** is data that takes a **non-numerical** or **unique value**, such as colours of cars and shoe sizes.

Example: The diagram shows the speeds of 100 cars on the B1026 and 100 cars on the M1. Comment on the differences in the two distributions.

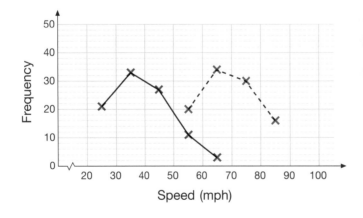

Key:
——— B1026
------- M1

The diagrams show that the two distributions have similar shapes but the speeds of the motorway are about 30 mph higher on average.

Top Tip!

If you are asked to compare distributions, comment on the shape, the spread (if it is significantly different) and the average values. The average will be in about the middle of the distribution.

Stem-and-leaf diagrams

- A **stem-and-leaf diagram** shows **ordered** data in a **concise** way.

Example: Show the data 32, 41, 56, 37, 38, 29, 42, 46, 38, 28, 34, 38, 37, 51, 49
on a stem-and-leaf diagram.

The **stem** is the **10s digit** and the **leaves** are the **units**.

```
2 | 8   9
3 | 2   4   7   7   8   8   8
4 | 1   2   6   9
5 | 1   6
```

Key: 2 | 8 represents 28

> **Top Tip!**
> Always put a **key** on a stem-and-leaf diagram.

Sample National Test question

The frequency diagram shows the number of lengths 20 students
swam in a sponsored swim.

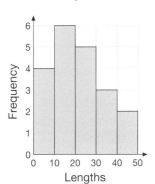

a How many students swam more than 20 lengths?

b The teacher wants to know the greatest number of
lengths that anyone swam.

Tick the correct box:

☐ 50   ☐ 40   ☐ 45   ☐ Cannot tell

Explain your answer.

Answers

a   5 students swam between 20 and 30 lengths, 3 swam between 30 and 40
lengths and 2 swam between 40 and 50 lengths. This is a total of 10 students.

b   Cannot tell. All you know is that 3 students swam between 40 and 50 lengths,
not how many lengths they swam.

> *Did YOU Know?*
> A Blue Whale's belly button is about 8 inches wide.

Spot Check

1 Put the following data under the correct headings in the table:
height of boys aged 15; marks in a spelling test out of 10; makes of
cars; number of matches in 10 boxes; time taken to run 100 metres.

Discrete data	Continuous data

HANDLING DATA   Scatter diagrams

Scatter diagrams

- A **scatter diagram** shows the relationship between two variables, for example: the temperature and the sales of ice cream.
- The mathematical name for the relationship is **correlation**.

The following diagrams show the different types of correlation.

  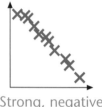

| Strong, positive correlation | Weak, positive correlation | No correlation | Weak, negative correlation | Strong, negative correlation |

Example: The scatter on the right diagram shows the relationship between the cost of taxi fares and distances of journeys.

a Describe the correlation between the variables.

b Describe the expected correlation between the following:
  i The cost of a taxi journey and the age of the taxi driver.
  ii The time of a taxi journey and the number of cars on the road.
  iii The distance of a taxi journey and the time of the journey.

a The diagram shows weak, positive correlation.

b *i* There will be no correlation between the age of a driver and the cost of a journey.

  ii The time of a taxi journey will increase with more cars on the road, so it would show weak, positive correlation.

  iii The longer a journey, the more time it would take so there is positive correlation.

Line of best fit

- A **line of best fit** is a line that passes through the data and passes as close to as many of the points as possible. It can be used to predict values.

Example: This scatter diagram shows the top speed and engine size of some cars, and a line of best fit.

a What does the scatter diagram show about the relationship between the engine size and top speed of cars?

b The top speed of a car is 120 mph. Use the line of best fit to estimate the engine size.

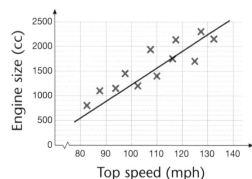

a The scatter diagram shows that cars with a larger engine have a higher top speed.

b Going up from 120 mph on the Top speed axis to the line of best fit and across to the Engine size axis gives 1900 cc.

Sample mental test question

Describe the correlation in the diagram.

The correlation is weak negative but you would still get marks for writing 'negative correlation'.

level
6

Sample National Test question

A fish breeder keeps records of the age and mass of his prize carp. He plots the results on a scatter diagram.

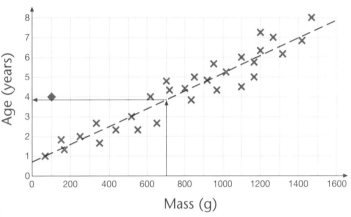

Mass (g)

a A fish is 4 years old and weighs 100 g.
Explain why this fish is not likely to be a carp.

b The breeder is given a carp that weighs 700 g but he does not know how old it is.
He only uses fish for breeding if they are over 5 years old. Will this fish be suitable for breeding?
Give a reason for your answer.

Answers

a *The data shows strong positive correlation.*
Plot the point (100, 4). (This is shown as a diamond.)
It is clear that this point is well away from the others. It does not have the same correlation as the other values so the fish is unlikely to be a carp.

b *Draw the line of best fit. (This is shown dashed.)*
Draw a line from 700 g up to the line of best fit and then across to the Age axis. (These are the solid lines.)
This comes to just under 4 years.
Therefore the fish may not be old enough for breeding.

Did YOU Know?
A human can jump about four times their body length. A flea can jump 350 times its body length.

Spot Check

1 Describe the expected correlation between:
   a the temperature and the number of cold drinks sold
   b the time of a journey and the average speed.

HANDLING DATA Surveys

Surveys

- **Surveys** are used to find out information. Groups, such as the government, need information so they can plan for the future. Companies need to know who buys their products.
- Information is usually collected using a **questionnaire**.
- For example, if you want to find out if students would like to have a party, you would want to know what day they would prefer, what type of refreshments, what type of music and how much they would pay.

- Questions in a questionnaire should be **unbiased**.

Example: This is a question on a survey about which day to hold a party.

You would prefer a party on Friday, wouldn't you?

Yes ☐   No ☐

This question is biased as it forces an opinion on the person being surveyed.

A better question would be:

On which day would you prefer a party?

Thursday ☐   Friday ☐   Saturday ☐

Top Tip!

Don't ask personal questions such as 'How old are you?' and expect an answer. People may be embarrassed to give their age.

Response sections

- Questions should have a simple response section with clear choices, no overlapping responses and a wide range of responses.

Example: Look at this question from a survey with a response section.

How old are you?

Under 10 ☐   10–20 ☐   20–30 ☐   Over 30 ☐

The response section of this question has overlapping categories.

A better question would be:

How old are you?

Under 10 ☐   11–20 ☐   21–30 ☐   31 or over ☐

Top Tip!

Keep questions short and with a small choice of answers. Make your responses simple so you can use tick boxes.

Sampling

- You also need to be very careful about where you undertake a survey and who you ask.

  If the school has a Friday lunchtime party and you did your survey there, you would get a **biased sample** as the students are likely to say 'yes'.

  If you just asked a Year 7 tutor group, they might not want a party and the views of the Year 11s would not have been taken into account. This would be a **non-representative sample**.

- You should make sure the people who are surveyed are from a range of age groups and have **different views**.

Top Tip!

One way to ensure an unbiased and representative sample is to choose the people you survey **randomly**. For example, you could put all the names in a hat and draw some out. In a **random sample** everyone has an **equal chance** of being picked for the sample.

Sample National Test question

Year 9 are planning a trip and some students decide to do a survey about where people want to go.

a This is one of Ricky's questions.

Do you want to go paintballing?

Yes ☐ No ☐

What is wrong with this question?

b This is another question.

How much are you willing to spend?

£0–£10 ☐ £0–£15 ☐ Over £20 ☐

What is wrong with this question?

c Ricky decides to ask all the boys in his football practice group.
What is wrong with this method of doing the survey?

Answers
a *There are not enough choices. Ricky is probably trying to get everyone to agree to go paintballing.*
b *The responses overlap so someone wanting to spend £9 would have two boxes to tick.*
c *They will all have similar opinions. The sample is non-representative and will give a biased response.*

Did You Know?

The first public opinion surveys started in 1935 and the first question ever asked was: 'Do you think expenditures by the government for relief and recovery are too little, too great, or just about right?'. You could find several things wrong with this question!

Spot Check

1 Give two reasons why this is not a good question in a survey:
'Fast food makes you fat and is unhealthy. Do you agree?'

Yes ☐ No ☐

The probability scale

- **Probability** is the **chance** that something will happen.
- An event that is **impossible** has a probability of 0.
  An event that is **certain** has a probability of 1.
  All other probabilities are between 0 and 1.
- The probability scale runs from 0 to 1.
- Various words can be used to describe probability such as:
  impossible, very unlikely, unlikely, evens, likely, very likely and certain.
  On a probability scale these would be:

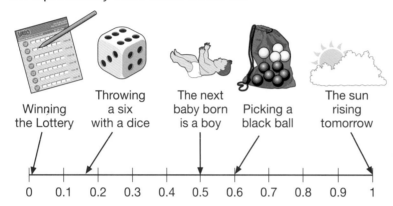

Winning the Lottery | Throwing a six with a dice | The next baby born is a boy | Picking a black ball | The sun rising tomorrow

0   0.1   0.2   0.3   0.4   0.5   0.6   0.7   0.8   0.9   1

Example: A bag contains 7 blue balls and 1 red ball.

a Imat is going to take a ball at random from the bag.

He says, 'There are two colours so it is equally likely that I will take a blue ball as a red ball'.

Explain why Imat is wrong.

b Complete the following sentences using the words below:

> impossible   very unlikely   unlikely   evens   likely   very likely   certain

A ball is taken at random from the bag.
The probability of taking a blue ball is ....
The probability of taking a green ball is ....

c How many red balls must be put in the bag to make the chance of taking a red ball evens?

a There are unequal numbers of each colour in the bag.
The probability of blue is $\frac{7}{8}$ and red is $\frac{1}{8}$.

b The probability of getting a blue ball is **very likely**.
The probability of getting a green ball is **impossible**.

c To make the probability evens, there should be the same number of each colour.
So 6 red balls need to be added.

Probability of events

- The total probability of all possible events is 1.
- These are examples of **mutually exclusive** events:

  P(boy) + P(girl) = 1

  P(head) + P(tail) = 1.

  The probability of an event is P(event) = $\dfrac{\text{number of ways event can happen}}{\text{number of total outcomes}}$

Example: **a** If the chance of picking a black ball from the bag shown here is $\frac{6}{10}$ or $\frac{3}{5}$, what is the chance of picking a white ball?

a You can see that there are four white balls so the chance of picking a white ball is $\frac{4}{10}$ or $\frac{2}{5}$.

Note that $\frac{6}{10} + \frac{4}{10} = 1$ and $\frac{3}{5} + \frac{2}{5} = 1$

Unless the question asks for an answer in 'its simplest form', you do not have to cancel fractions, but be careful if you do.

Top Tip!

You need to add up the total number of balls to find the denominator of the fraction.

Sample National Test question

A box of juice drinks contains four orange, three grapefruit, two cranberry and one lemon drink. A drink is taken at random from the box.

a What is the probability it is orange?

b What is the probability that it is not lemon?

c Priti drinks two orange juices. She then takes a drink at random from the remaining drinks. What is the probability she takes a cranberry juice?

Answers

a P(orange) = $\frac{4}{10}$ = $\frac{2}{5}$

b P(not lemon) = $\frac{9}{10}$

c There are only 8 drinks left, 2 are cranberry.

   P(cranberry) = $\frac{2}{8}$ = $\frac{1}{4}$

Top Tip!

There are 9 out of 10 that are not lemon but it can also be worked out as

1 − P(lemon)

$1 - \frac{1}{10} = \frac{9}{10}$

Did You Know?

The probability of winning the lottery is 1 in 14 million.

Spot Check

1 A bag contains 4 red counters and 8 blue counters. A counter is taken out at random.

What is the probability that the counter is: **a** red **b** blue **c** green?

Probability

- The probability of an event is the number of ways that event can happen divided by the total number of outcomes.

  Consider throwing a two on a dice. There is one way of throwing a two, and six ways the dice can land, so P(2 with a dice) = $\frac{1}{6}$.

Example: When a dice is thrown, what is the probability of:

a a score of 4   **b** a square number   **c** a factor of 24?

The dice can land six ways.

a There is only one 4 so P(4) = $\frac{1}{6}$

b Square numbers are 1 and 4, so P(square) = $\frac{2}{6}$ = $\frac{1}{3}$

c The factors of 24 on a dice are 1, 2, 3, 4, 6 so

P(factors of 24) = $\frac{5}{6}$

Example: A box contains 21 copper nails and 9 steel nails.

A nail is taken out at random.

a What is the probability that it is a copper nail?

Give your answer as a fraction in its simplest form.

b Give your answer to part **a** as a percentage.

c The first nail is put back in the box. Then six nails are taken out of the box.

After the nails are removed, the probability of taking a copper nail at random is $\frac{7}{8}$.

Explain how you know that the six nails taken out were steel nails.

a P(copper) = $\frac{21}{30}$ = $\frac{7}{10}$

b $\frac{7}{10}$ = 70%

c There are now 24 nails in the box.

If P(copper) = $\frac{7}{8}$ = $\frac{21}{24}$, then there are still 21 copper nails in the box.

So the nails removed must have been steel nails.

Top Tip!

You need to know the equivalent decimals and percentages for some simple fractions

 **Spot Check**

1 A bag contains 6 red, 4 blue and 10 green balls. A ball is taken out at random.

What is the probability that the ball is:

a red   **b** green   **c** not blue?

2 The word 'statistics' is spelled out on cards.

The cards are shuffled and one is chosen at random.

What is the probability that:

a it is the letter I

b it is an S or a T

c it is one of the letters in the word CAST?

Combined events

- Sometimes two separate events can take place at the same time; for example, throwing a dice and tossing a coin.
- The mathematical name for events like this is **independent**, because the outcome of throwing the dice does not have any influence on the outcome of tossing the coin.
- The combined outcomes of the two events can be shown in different ways.
- They can be written as a **list**:

(1, head), (1, tail), (2, head), (2, tail), (3, head), (3, tail),

(4, head), (4, tail), (5, head), (5, tail), (6, head), (6, tail)

- They can also be shown in a **sample space** diagram:
- You can see that there are 12 outcomes for the **combined events**.

To work out the probability of throwing a head with the coin and a square number on the dice, you would need to count which of the 12 outcomes satisfy the conditions.

These are shown in a box on the sample space diagram. So P(head and square number) = $\frac{2}{12} = \frac{1}{6}$

Sample mental test question

A box of toffee contains hard and soft toffees only. The probability of taking a hard toffee is $\frac{8}{15}$. What is the probability of taking a soft toffee?

The probability of a hard toffee is $\frac{8}{15}$, so the probability of a soft toffee is $1 - \frac{8}{15} = \frac{7}{15}$.

Sample National Test question

Two four-sided dice numbered from 1 to 4 are thrown together. The scores are multiplied together.

a Complete the sample space diagram showing the possible scores of the combined event.

b Find the probability that the combined score is:

  i an even number   **ii** a square number   **iii** a factor of 144.

Answers

a

Score on second dice	1	2	3	4
1	1	2	3	4
2	2	4	6	8
3	3	6	9	12
4	4	8	12	16

b **i** There are 16 outcomes and 12 of them are even numbers. P(even) = $\frac{12}{16} = \frac{3}{4}$

ii There are 6 square numbers: 1, 4, 4, 4, 9, 16. P(square) = $\frac{6}{16} = \frac{3}{8}$

iii All of the numbers are factors of 144. P(factor of 144) = 1

Did You Know? If you are in a room with 30 strangers, the chance that one of them has the same birthday as you is over a half.

Index